Adam Smith

Profiles in
Economics

Milton Friedman

John Maynard Keynes

Karl Marx

Adam Smith

Profiles in
Economics

Adam Smith

Cynthia D. Crain and Dwight R. Lee

MORGAN
REYNOLDS
PUBLISHING

Greensboro, NC

Dedication:
Our thanks and appreciation to James Buchanan,
Anna and Robert Tollison, Jane Shaw, John
Morton, Eugene Miller, and David Robinson

BC#34896 92
SMI

Morgan Reynolds Publishing
620 South Elm Street, Suite 387
Greensboro, NC 27406
www.morganreynolds.com
1-800-535-1504

First printing

1 3 5 7 9 8 6 4 2

Library of Congress Cataloging-in-Publication Data

Crain, Cynthia D.
 Profiles in economics : Adam Smith / by Cynthia D. Crain and Dwight R. Lee.
  p. cm. — (Profiles in economics)
 Includes bibliographical references and index.
 ISBN-13: 978-1-59935-107-0
 ISBN-10: 1-59935-107-2
 1. Smith, Adam, 1723-1790. 2. Economists—Scotland—Biography. I. Lee,
Dwight R. II. Title.
 HB103.S6C67 2009
 330.15'3092—dc22
 [B]
                                                    2009000138

TABLE OF CONTENTS

The Young Smith

Adam Smith was born in Scotland in June 1723. Named after his late father who had died at the age of forty-four shortly before his son's birth, Adam and his mother lived in the small seaport town of Kirkcaldy in the Burgh of Fife, where there was a windy and gray spring rainy season and homes were smoky from the indoor wood fires necessary for heating and cooking. Growing up in this damp coastal climate, Adam's "constitution during infancy was infirm and sickly, and required all the tender solicitude of his surviving parent," wrote a family friend, Dugald Stewart.

Adam's father had been a widower with a young son when he met his future wife, Margaret Douglas, through her brother, Robert Douglas. Robert, the heir of the Douglas family estate, was a laird with tenant farmers to manage. Some other men in Margaret's family held various military positions. Women often married in their teens, but Margaret was already in her twenties when she married Smith and left the family home in Strathendry, Scotland, to live with her husband and eleven-year-old stepson, Hugh, in nearby Kirkcaldy.

Born near Aberdeen, Scotland, in 1679, Adam Smith Sr. had been educated and trained as a lawyer. Early in his professional career he worked for a nobleman, the Earl of Loudon, who later assisted Smith in obtaining a highly sought-after job as a comptroller of customs in Kirkcaldy. Although Smith was neither a nobleman nor independently wealthy, his government job of enforcing trade laws and collecting taxes made him an important man in the Burgh of Fife. The position provided the Smith family a regular and secure salary, and it came with perks, such as bonuses from the king. When Smith died three years after marrying Margaret, he left his family a secure and comfortable income, although they were not wealthy.

A nineteenth-century view of Kirkcaldy, the Scottish town where Adam Smith was born.

Margaret Douglas Smith was widowed a few weeks before giving birth to her son, Adam. She was criticized for indulging Adam during his childhood. The two would remain very close until her death at age ninety.

Scottish funerals were expensive, though. About 1,500 people resided in Kirkcaldy, and custom required that every citizen be invited to the home of the deceased. A church officer ringing a bell announced the death. Visitors would then join the family to view the coffin and pay their respects, and custom required that the family purchase food and drink—cakes and bread, ale and liquor, as well as tobacco—to serve to any visitor who dropped by the house. In addition to paying for food and drink, Margaret Smith also had to pay for the burial services, which included twenty-eight pounds sterling (£28) for making the coffin and £3 for digging the grave. She also gave a donation of £3 to the poor. The mourners dressed in black, so Margaret had to buy proper clothes for her family as well. The funeral expenses cost Margaret about £80; Smith's annual salary had been £40 a year. The cost of the funeral was almost twice Smith's salary for one year.

With her stepson Hugh living at a boarding school, Margaret had to raise her infant son, Adam, almost alone. Fortunately, Kirkcaldy wasn't far from her family home in Strathendry, and her brother Robert and his family provided some support and assistance.

When he was three years old, Adam went missing from outside the Douglas family house, where he had been playing. Robert and Margaret soon discovered that Adam had been kidnapped by a group of vagrants referred to as tinkers. Because of their nomadic lifestyles, many tinkers were beggars and petty thieves, and some kidnapped children to sell them into slavery. Luckily, Uncle Robert found Adam near Leslie wood, and brought him home safely.

The town of Kirkcaldy had become a royal burgh (similar to a parish or a county) in 1644 when granted a charter of confirmation by the king of Scotland, Charles I. In the 1700s Scotland was divided into two sections—highlands and lowlands. Kirkcaldy, located along the bay of the Firth of Forth on the lower eastern side of the country, is in the lowlands. Scots were either highlanders or lowlanders, and Adam and his family were lowlanders.

Lowlanders in the 1700s shared social customs more in line with the English than with their brethren living up north. Looking much like the English in fashion and style, lowlander women wore simple dresses that were plain and practical for cooking and cleaning. Married women often wore plain colored bonnets on their heads, which distinguished them from young bareheaded women who were single. Lowlander gentlemen wore white wigs sprinkled with hair powder, and often carried a staff when walking about town. Male clothing consisted of a simple coat-jacket of blue, gray, or brown, over a light-colored shirt. Their stockings were light colored, and shoes were leather boots or flats

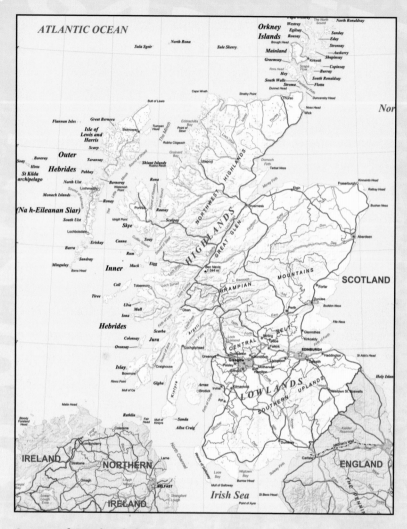

A map of Scotland showing the Highlands and the Lowlands.

adorned with ornamental big buckles. Gentlemen wore cocked hats and boys wore velvet caps.

Fertile farmlands and bustling seaports were found in the lowlands, and although the economy of Scotland in general was much less prosperous than that of England and France, people in the lowlands lived under better conditions than those in the sparsely populated highlands.

Living in the lowlands, Adam and his mother could have their choice of herring, eel, or oysters from the sea, as well as beef, chicken, pigeons, or pork from the farms, boiled with fresh vegetables and spiced with parsley and cinnamon. A special delicacy was mutton boiled with cauliflowers, turnips and carrots. They often ate haggis (a mixture of animal parts such as heart, liver, and lungs, seasoned with onions, oatmeal, and spices, and boiled in the stomach of the slaughtered animal). Cheese and fruit, especially strawberries, were favorites of Adam.

This 1738 portrait of an upper-class English family shows common fashions of the time.

Although Scotland was not as culturally advanced as other countries in Europe, the arts—music, theater, painting, and architecture—were developing in the lowlands. Major universities (for men only) had been established in the lowland cities of Aberdeen, Glasgow, and Edinburgh. Students received a broad education in science, mathematics, jurisprudence, history, ethics, and philosophy, and pursued degrees in medicine, law, or divinity.

Like most lowlanders, Adam and his family were Presbyterians, while most highlanders were Catholic. Unlike other parts of Europe at the time, the Scottish church (or the kirk, as the Scots called it) was strongly opposed to the movement toward greater religious toleration, and Presbyterianism was practically the only reli-

A nineteenth-century view of Glasgow, with the Presbyterian Glasgow Cathedral at center. During Smith's time, the Presbyterian Church had great influence in the Scottish Lowlands.

gion allowed in the lowland cities, such as Kirkcaldy. The Presbyterian Church played an important role in the day-to-day activities of the Scots, with government and religion closely connected.

Church officials filled some of the positions on town councils and monitored all aspects of society's activities, including dispensing punishment for breaking the law. Church law mandated that every citizen attend church on Sundays, and this law was strictly enforced. Individuals were assigned to check homes, taverns, and coffee and chocolate houses to make certain that no one missed church services without a good excuse. The punishment for breaking this law was harsh, with the disobedient man or woman usually taken to the center of town and forced to sit on an uncomfortable stool for repentance—in full view of the public.

The Church required that schoolboys meet every Sunday for a day of activities together. Beginning at nine in the morning they met with the chaplain for religious studies on the Bible and to learn the rules of good behavior. Then they attended church service from ten to twelve-thirty. Because the church did not allow people to cook on Sundays (or even pluck a chicken), people ate a cold lunch from twelve-thirty to two in the afternoon. The schoolboys brought their lunches and ate together instead of joining their families. Following lunch, the schoolboys would gather with all children—boys and girls ages two to five—and servants to meet with the chaplain to test their religious knowledge. Finally at six in the evening, the schoolboys were allowed to go home to their families for a cold dinner.

After a light supper families would sing religious songs, read from the Bible, and pray together.

Church law also mandated and enforced public education. In 1696 the Scottish Parliament had passed the Act for Setting Schools that required every burgh to supply a school building and financially provide for a teacher to educate young boys. Girls studied elsewhere, usually at home, where they were instructed in such activities as sewing, knitting, spinning, and rudimentary reading. The reason for this act was that the church assembly wanted its male constituents to learn to read, especially the scriptures. By the time Adam started school in 1729 at the age of six, the literacy rate for males had greatly increased, at least in the lowlands. In the highlands, where governmental laws were more difficult to enforce, the literacy rate was lower.

Adam's day at the Burgh School of Kirkcaldy near his house was almost as long as Sunday religious services. The school had two classrooms, with about thirty boys assigned to each room. He and the others arrived early in the morning to begin their studies of Greek and Latin languages, classical literature, and general reading, writing, and arithmetic. They learned Scottish folk and religious songs. Students brought their lunch to school and did not return home until late in the afternoon.

In 1734, the Kirkcaldy Town Council, upon deciding that a more extensive education was important for their boys, recruited David Millar, a teacher with an exceptional reputation, to take the headmaster position at the Burgh School. Following custom the boys' families were expected to pay—based on their financial circumstances—

most of Millar's salary. With Millar as headmaster of the school all boys living in Kirkcaldy, both rich and poor, had the opportunity for an excellent education.

Adam's friends at school and home included the Oswald brothers—John and older brother James—whose father owned an estate with a nail-making business. Also, there were John and George Drysdale, sons of a minister. When the weather was good the boys played outdoor sports—running games, archery, tennis, and golf were favorites. In winter they played ice-skating games. Adam, however, was not physically strong enough to play most sports; he was frail and clumsy. He much preferred reading.

Books were expensive and difficult to find in Kirkcaldy, though, so Adam had to borrow from friends and family. There was no public library and no bookstores, although occasionally a shopkeeper kept a few books to sell or loan. The books Adam did manage to read were of famous philosophers, such as Aristotle, Plato, and Epictetus. As he grew older and became fluent in both Greek and Latin, he read classic histories of ancient Greek and Roman societies. He also read literature, including Shakespeare's *Macbeth* and John Milton's *Paradise Lost*.

When not reading, Adam liked to observe people. He and his mother lived in town close to the port, so he had many opportunities to watch people trading. From his favorite spot high on a steep hill on the outskirts of the small town, he sat and watched people hustling around the active port. He even carried a pen and notebook to record his observations, thoughts, and questions as he watched men and women go about their day-to-day business. Much of what he saw traded was smuggled goods.

Throughout the seventeenth century the Scots and the English had shared a monarch while maintaining independent parliaments—the English Parliament that resided in London and the Scottish Parliament in Edinburgh. Because the English monarch and his Parliament had more authority than the Scottish parliament, laws were enforced on Scotland that the Scots believed to be unfair—such as trade restrictions. This uneven balance of power had caused many conflicts between the two countries and had encouraged the smuggling trade in Scotland.

Then between 1697 and 1703 the Scots suffered famine from at least three crop failures and the economy of Scotland went from poor to bad. The Scottish parliament believed that if it convinced England to lessen trade restrictions, the economy would improve. The English parliament, taking advantage of the Scots' predicament, agreed to lessen the trade restrictions under the condition that the Scottish parliament would agree to an official Treaty of Union with England and then disband. The Scottish parliament, finding no other option to save its country, agreed to the Union by a vote of 110 to sixty-seven. As the English had promised, the Union of 1707 gave Scotland the opportunity for more trade with the colonies, and the Scots gained a few seats in the English parliament at the price of their own parliament and independence.

Most Scots detested what the Scottish parliament had done. They resented losing their Parliament and viewed the merger as a takeover rather than a union. They feared they would lose their history and culture, and that they'd be forced to accept the Church of England.

The Scottish parliament had been correct, though, that a lessening of trade restrictions would be beneficial. When Scotland began to engage in profitable trade with the English colonies—particularly the American and Indian colonies—the Scottish economy improved. However, there were still restrictions and tariff duties imposed on imports, especially on imports from non-British markets, and much of the tariff revenues went to England rather than Scotland.

The improving economy did not appease the Anti-Unionist Scots in either the lowlands or highlands. They did not want to be ruled by the English parliament and complained about having to pay taxes to Great Britain. When the English parliament assessed a tax on malt and salt, there was a riot in Scotland's second-largest city, Glasgow, and the demand for beer decreased and whisky increased. Even though the Union had improved the overall economy, by 1730 smuggling had become common as a way to acquire cheap products from other countries and avoid paying tariff revenues to England. Nearly everyone in Kirkcaldy and other Scottish ports—including bakers, shoemakers, schoolmasters, fisher-men, and lairds—trafficked in smuggled goods.

Smuggling went on during all hours of the day. French sailors hauled oils and wines to the Kirkcaldy shore during the day to trade for goods such as salt and nails. At night, white sheets and small fires lit the dark-ness across the hilly coast, signaling French and Danish seamen where to come ashore. There was even the Hell-fire Club—a local Scottish organization that promoted smuggling.

Adam spent hours observing the hustle and bustle of people trading and smuggling. He knew that the rebellious Anti-Unionists were pleased that Scottish citizens defied the English king and Parliament and risked trading with countries outside Great Britain, such as Denmark and France. People boasted that barely one-third of the tea brought to the Scottish shores by a foreign ship ever made it to the customs house in Kirkcaldy to be taxed.

Adam also witnessed briberies: smugglers paid money, perfume, or perhaps a few furs to the tax collector to avoid being fined or jailed. On occasion, the tax collector would arrest a smuggler to make the king think that he was doing his job. As a reward, the king would

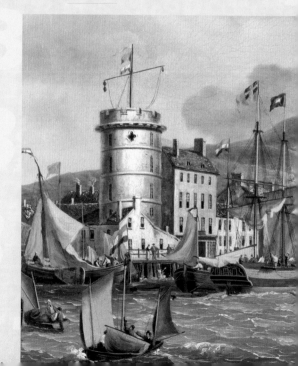

Leith Harbor in Scotland, early 1800s. As Adam was growing up, one of his favorite pastimes was to observe port activity.

then pay the tax collector a bonus for each arrest. In the meantime, the smuggler would pay his fine, and perhaps pay the tax collector a little extra, and be free to come back to Scotland to smuggle another day.

Because customs taxes were a major source of revenue for Scotland and England, customs collectors had an important governmental role in enforcing trade laws and punishing tax evaders. Adam was very familiar with the job of custom collector: his cousin Hercules Scott Smith and his father both had served as tax collectors in Kirkcaldy.

Out the back window of his house, Adam saw ships in the bay exporting salt, coal, and nails, and importing scrap iron for nail-making. Nails were an important export for Scotland because they were in demand throughout Europe for shipbuilding. Adam was fascinated with the process of nail-making. Along with his

A blacksmith makes nails on an anvil. Nails were an important export for Scotland, and Adam was fascinated by the nail-making process.

friends, John and James Oswald, he watched workmen make nails in the nail-making shop on the Oswald estate. Adam thought the nail-making process "by no means one of the simplest operations. The same person blows the bellows, stirs or mends the fire as there is occasion, heats the iron, and forges every part of the nail."

Through the age of thirteen, Adam studied hard. According to Dugald Stewart, Adam "attracted notice, by his passion for books, and by the extraordinary powers of his memory." Although he sometimes talked to himself out loud and was sometimes absentminded, he was appreciated for his good-humored nature. Even though poor health prevented him from participating in games and sports with his more active schoolmates, he was well liked. Because he showed an excellent memory for facts and dates, he was asked by his schoolmates to help them with their schoolwork, especially mathematics.

The church taught that the salvation of a child depended on discipline and that parents must use authority and fear to win obedience and their children's love. Usually Margaret Smith was a strict, dedicated follower of the church, yet she chose tolerance in raising her son and consequently was criticized for being too lenient in disciplining Adam. "She was blamed for treating him with an unlimited indulgence; but it produced no unfavourable effects on his temper or his dispositions," Stewart recalled.

At the age of fourteen, Adam was considered a man in the custom of eighteenth-century Scotland. An uncle and three cousins on his mother's side of the family were military officers. Another uncle ran the Douglas farming estate. Adam's health would not allow him to serve in the military or to manage a large farm. It was obvious that he was very intelligent, excellent at reading and writing. The most common choice for such a scholarly person at the time was to get educated and become a minister. Though Adam could have married at age fourteen (brides were frequently as young as twelve), Adam instead chose to reject a young lady he'd been interested in and attend the University of Glasgow to hopefully receive a scholarship to study for the ministry.

2 College Years

In 1737, Adam Smith left his family and friends in Kirkcaldy and moved to Glasgow, the second-largest city in Scotland, to attend college. Boys usually matriculated college at age twelve, but Adam was fourteen because he had started school late due to his frail health. Traveling by boat, he crossed the bay of the Firth of Forth to Edinburgh, the largest city in Scotland, which had been the home of the Scottish parliament until the Union of 1707. Smith rode a horse across Scotland from Edinburgh to Glasgow—few horse-drawn carriages traveled between towns because roads were nothing more than narrow dirt paths and constant rain kept them muddy.

Glasgow was home to more than 15,000 people, considerably more than the 2,000 who lived in Kirkcaldy. Located in the western part of the country on the Atlantic Ocean it had a bustling port filled with ships, filled with cargo. Many more ships came to Glasgow's port than Kirkcaldy's, especially ships from Canada and North America, and because of the growing tobacco trade with the American colonies, Glasgow merchants saw their businesses and wealth increasing rapidly.

Smith found the move to the University of Glasgow an exciting adventure. He now had ready access to a library filled with books, and was able to attend interesting classes taught by professors who were famous enough to attract students from all over Europe. Two of these well-known professors were Alexander Dunlop, professor of Greek, and Robert Simson, professor of mathematics.

Smith also studied under Dr. Francis Hutcheson, a former Presbyterian minister from Ireland. Since the fall of 1730, Dr. Hutcheson, the professor of moral philosophy, had been teaching and serving on every major

A nineteenth-century view of Glasgow. Adam moved from Kirkcaldy to Glasgow in 1737 to attend college.

The University of Glasgow, where Adam studied under several notable professors.

committee at the university. When Smith began his studies, the forty-three-year-old Dr. Hutcheson was actively engaged in writing for literary publications like the *Dublin Journal* and using his classroom to explain and explore ideas for improving society. The university was considered an appendage of the Presbytery, and every professor had to sign the Confession of Faith before beginning his job, but signing this document did not deter Dr. Hutcheson from expressing his sometimes controversial ideas. From Hutcheson's lectures, Smith learned about the Enlightenment and the power of ideas to improve the lives of ordinary people.

The Age of Enlightenment was an intellectual movement that began in the mid-1600s, continued through the American Revolution of 1776, and ended with the French Revolution around the middle of the 1790s. Technological improvements throughout Europe—such as the invention of moveable type and the printing press—greatly contributed to the Enlightenment by allowing new knowledge to spread more rapidly among educated men and women and by increasing the number of people receiving an education.

The scholarly leaders of the Enlightenment had become known as the literati. As the Enlightenment progressed, many in the literati argued that ordinary people could be depended upon to think for themselves, rather than relying on religious and political authorities to do the thinking for them. They believed that ordinary people should be given more freedom. This was far from the dominant view among the upper classes and religious and political authorities, however.

A 1745 portrait of Dr. Francis Hutcheson, long-time professor of moral philosophy at the University of Glasgow and one of the leading figures of the Scottish Enlightenment. Hutcheson would have considerable influence on the thought of his student Adam Smith.

In an era when free speech was largely unprotected and political and religious authorities had a large amount of control over people, even the idea that desirable outcomes could emerge from widespread freedom was controversial. But many literati were willing to follow the logic of their ideas where it took them and state their conclusions despite the risk of upsetting people in power.

As time passed members of the literati began to grow in number and increase their representation in church and Parliament, and some had become part of the elite class. Not surprisingly, opposing factions had formed within the literati, with the differing sides growing strident in voicing their conflicting views on ideas such as how society should progress and on what laws to change. The disagreements had occasionally become violent. In the late 1600s, certain members of the literati had suffered exile, or worse, for upsetting authorities.

Three members of the literati—the Earl of Shaftesbury, Algernon Sidney, and John Locke—were persecuted for writing, among other things, that the purpose of government (the king and Parliament) was to serve the interest of the people, and that a government that failed to do so could be legitimately overthrown. For advancing these views openly, the three were condemned by the king in 1683 for committing treason. The Earl of Shaftesbury, who had been imprisoned in the Tower of London, escaped and fled to the more tolerant Dutch city of Amsterdam. Leaving his wife and children behind in England, he took ill and died alone in Holland. He also left behind his friend, Algernon Sidney, who was also imprisoned in the Tower of

John Locke, a prominent Enlightenment philosopher, advocated the separation of church and state.

London awaiting trial. Unable to win his case against the crown, on December 7, 1683, Sidney was taken from the Tower to the scaffold. After paying his executioner five guineas, he was beheaded. John Locke, whose ideas would have an important influence upon the founders of the United States of America, went into self-exile in Holland, fleeing for his life after seeing what had happened to Shaftesbury and Sidney.

While the English government in the late 1600s often used laws against treason to restrain men and women in voicing their controversial opinions, the Presbyterian Church in Scotland threatened people with the charge of heresy. A notable example involved Thomas Aikenhead, a student at Edinburgh University in 1696 studying to become a minister. One night while out drinking with friends, Aikenhead supposedly made jokes questioning God's existence and the authority of the church to dictate people's religious beliefs. Although it is not certain whether Aikenhead meant the things he said, when the Edinburgh town council and church heard about Aikenhead's comments he was jailed and charged for breaking two laws: denying God's existence and cursing God, the latter a crime punishable by death. The Lord Advocate in Edinburgh chose to prosecute the case and make an example of Aikenhead. The case went to trial and Aikenhead was judged guilty; the punishment was death.

Appalled by the government's actions, some members of the literati risked punishment to defend Aikenhead. John Locke, who believed in the separation of church and state, wrote that religious belief should be a personal, private matter and without interference from any public authority. In Scotland, where so-called witches were still prosecuted and punished by death in 1696, these appeals did not save Thomas Aikenhead. In January 1697, the eighteen-year-old student was taken to the public gallows and hanged.

But the Enlightenment would not die. Thinkers and writers continued to join the movement. By the time Smith attended the University of Glasgow in 1737, the literati had grown to become a new identifiable class in society, much different from the traditional classes of nobility, ministers, merchants, farmers, and peasants. The farmers had their fields, the nobility their castles and armies. The literati had their coffeehouses and alehouses, as well as an increasing number of clubs and universities, for challenging, refining, and sharing their ideas and arguments. Using the increasing availability of newspapers, pamphlets, and journals, and through open forums, they wrote and gave lectures. And slowly they had begun to influence the way ordinary people looked at the world.

In addition to learning about Dr. Hutcheson's views on freedom—which were similar to those of Shaftesbury, Sidney, and Locke—Smith was introduced to his theories of economics, and he found his teacher's lectures on the importance of trade particularly fascinating.

Walking along the busy Glasgow port, Smith observed firsthand how the tobacco trade with the American colonies was benefiting the fast-growing, wealthy Glasgow merchant class. Farming methods were also becoming more efficient and there had not been a bad harvest in the Scottish lowlands since the late 1600s. With increased agricultural productivity, fewer workers were needed on the farms, and cities such as Glasgow and Edinburgh were swelling in population as people moved from the countryside to take the increasing number of available jobs.

The growing economy had improved the living conditions for upper-class Scots. For those in the lower

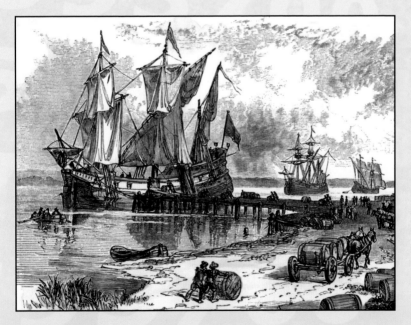

Barrels of tobacco are loaded onto ships in Virginia. By the 1700s, Scottish merchants were growing rich by importing tobacco from the American colonies.

The Scottish philosopher David Hume, author of *A Treatise of Human Nature*, became a close friend of Adam Smith.

classes, though, the standard of living had not changed much. They had good reason to believe that their situation would never change: no matter how much skill and talent they acquired, without connections to noblemen or the church, there was little chance for them to improve their conditions and status by saving, investing, and working hard.

Being curious and observant, Smith began to question the traditional customs and government policies that gave special privileges to a few at the expense of the greater part of the population. He questioned whether a nation could be considered truly prosperous without making full use of the skills and talents of ordinary men and women, and allowing them to improve their standard of living. Questions like these were already being considered and debated by the leaders in the Enlightenment, many of whom were Scots.

When Smith started studying at the University of Glasgow, enough Scottish intellectuals had become such influential members of the Enlightenment that Scotland had its own intellectual movement, the Scottish Enlightenment. Professor Hutcheson was a prominent member of the Scottish Enlightenment, along with the historian and philosopher David Hume. A third influential Scot was Judge Henry Home, known later in life as Lord Kames. These Scots, along with Europeans such as Bernard Mandeville, a Dutch physician, and the French philosophers, Baron de Montesquieu and Voltaire, were considering how people, regardless of their stations in life, could find it in their interest to behave in ways that would create a generally beneficial social order if given their natural right to freedom.

Dr. Hutcheson used his classroom to explain to his students why it was right to give men and women more freedom, and why more freedom could help everyone in society to be better off. The question in the minds of literati such as Hutcheson and his close friend Hume was not just why change was needed to allow people more freedom, but how and what kind of change. In talking with Dr. Hutcheson, Smith learned about the professor's beliefs, including the freedom of people of all social classes to own property; to choose occupations or go into businesses of their own without getting special permission; to trade with whoever offered them the best deal whether or not they were foreigners; and even to wear what they wanted (at one time there had been sumptuary laws preventing people in the lower classes from wearing the type of clothing worn by the nobility). Smith began to understand the need for change and the kinds of changes required.

But getting people and governments to change was not easy. For centuries ordinary people had grown accustomed to yielding to the political and religious authorities. The resistance to change came partly from inertia and partly from the interests of those in power.

Yet literati such as Hutcheson persisted in voicing their opinions, and one major change many of them recommended to advance the intellectual revolution was the separation of church and state.

Religious and political authorities had no interest in separating church and state. Government from the local town councils up through the ranks of Parliament and king were strongly influenced by church officials who for centuries had encouraged the belief that the social positions of people—from the woman living in the poorhouse to the king in his castle—were determined by God's will. With government and church working together, social mobility had been discouraged, limited by laws making it difficult for people in the lower classes to get jobs typically reserved for those in higher classes.

In Kirkcaldy, Smith had observed how the law and church limited people's social mobility in at least two different ways. First, he witnessed bondage, or slavery—men and women who bonded themselves for life to an owner of a salt pit or coal mine. Infants and children could be bonded without choice if an impoverished parent accepted the financial incentive offered by a mine owner to sell their infants into bondage for life. Such a child, once an adult, had no recourse; Scottish law protected a contract of bondage, and only the owner could end it. Second, Adam witnessed the practice of apprenticeship. If a twelve-year-old youth wanted to acquire the skills, say, of a blacksmith, he had first to get permission to work as an apprentice for an employer (under a contract) for a specified number of years. This limited his opportunities to take his skill and move elsewhere for higher pay. These apprentice contracts required that the youth work long hours for very low wages, which allowed the employer to profit from cheap labor for years. Government and church authorities saw nothing wrong with either bondage or apprenticeship. Restrictions on people's freedoms were not only God's will but necessary, they argued, to maintain a social order that benefited everyone.

Another major change being advocated by literati such as Hutcheson had to do with trade. Smith learned that merchants had been effective over the years at

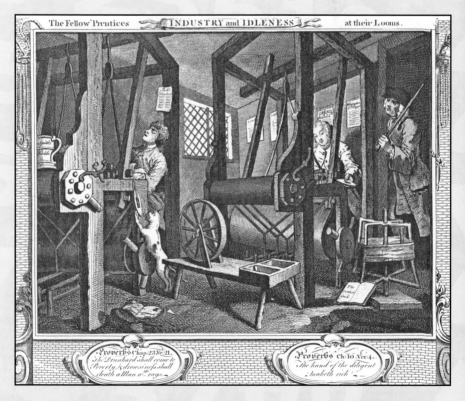

This 1747 illustration by William Hogarth shows two apprentices working at looms under the watchful eye of their master. Early on, Smith observed that the practice of apprenticeship limited a worker's freedom, mobility, and opportunity for higher wages.

getting laws passed making it possible for them to prof-it further by restricting imports—preventing people from buying products sold by foreign producers. In addition to laws making it difficult for Scots and others in Great Britain to buy products from foreign countries, mer-chants also had succeeded in getting laws passed that gave themselves special subsidies and assistance in selling their products to those countries. This policy of restricting trade, which brought more money into the country by selling exports than left the country from buying imports, was known as mercantilism.

In 1737, Hutcheson and Hume, along with other members of the literati, argued for a change in mercan-tilist laws to allow people more freedom to trade. Those who benefited from mercantilist policies argued that economic freedom would disrupt social order and bank-rupt the nation. Certain products like food, clothing, housing, and fuel had to be produced, and produced in the right amounts if people were to be fed, clothed, housed, and kept warm. They argued that if people were free to work in any occupation they wanted, there would be no way to make sure that they would not pro-duce more of some things that were needed and not enough of other things.

Regarding trade with other countries, mercantilists argued that a country gets wealthier only when more money comes into the country from exporting products than leaves the country from importing products. Similarly, a country gets poorer when more money leaves the country from importing than comes into the country from exporting. If people were free to import all they wanted from foreign countries, they might be better off in the short run, but what would prevent their imports from bankrupting their country in the long run?

Smith also learned about morality in society. In 1737, the commonly accepted view of morality dated back to the seventeenth century view spread by the writings of Thomas Hobbes. Hobbes, an English political philosopher, had argued that people were basically selfish, and therefore cooperation was impossible if people were free to pursue their own interests. Hobbes further argued that the only way to get people to treat each other with decency and to work together for the common good was by giving a powerful government (the king or queen) almost unlimited authority to make people behave in ways they would never choose on their own. In the eighteenth century, certain members of the literati, called Hobbesians, had perpetuated Hobbes' arguments.

Hutcheson and Hume did not agree with the Hobbesians. They wrote that men and women developed a moral sense through their interactions with each other—through cooperation—and that moral sense was one of the things that maintained social order without government forcing people to behave in ways specified by the authorities. They believed that most people had a natural sense of morality and virtue that allowed a social order to be maintained, and that society could benefit from more freedom. Still, most government and religious authorities were not convinced or ready to give up their authority, and they steadfastly held onto the Hobbesian view.

It was more than just Professor Hutcheson's enlightened teachings that impressed Smith; he was unlike any person Smith had ever known. Most professors at Scottish universities stood at the front of the room and read their lecture notes in Latin; Professor Hutcheson walked up and down the width of the room giving animated lectures from memory in English to a room filled with enthusiastic students. He gave additional Sunday lectures, and held private classes for local tradesmen. Lecturing in English allowed the sons of shopkeepers, who were not fluent in Latin, to understand the professor's lectures on religion and moral philosophy. While professors at Glasgow were reputed to maintain an aloofness from students, Dr. Hutcheson made himself available. It did not matter whether a student was specializing in the study of philosophy, mathematics, or divinity; Hutcheson believed his first priority was to mold a young man's character. His second priority was to teach, and his subjects covered everything from religion, morals, and jurisprudence, to economics and government. In Scotland, university students paid most of their professor's salary, and the teachers who taught well were paid well. Dr. Hutcheson's teaching ability made him popular and well paid.

Dr. Hutcheson sought to bring the Enlightenment to the University of Glasgow—attacking old traditions and promoting new ideas on how to improve society. While many students of Dr. Hutcheson's were grateful for this new light, the church and Presbytery university officials had quarrels with it, and ultimately, they were in charge. Contrary to the rigorous orthodoxy of the Presbytery,

Professor Hutcheson taught his students that serving the interests and promoting the happiness of others was a moral behavior and that people could have a strong sense of good and evil independent of their religious beliefs. The Presbytery of Glasgow prosecuted Professor Hutcheson for heresy and moved to have him fired from his professorship. At the trial a group of upper-class, tuition-paying students appeared before the authorities to defend their professor. Dr. Hutcheson was acquitted and his university position saved.

As a protégé of Dr. Hutcheson's, Smith had met someone who could help provide insight into the questions he had asked himself from his years of observations while growing up in Kirkcaldy. Were mercantilist laws that increased the cost of importing foreign products necessary? Given all the activity in port towns like Kirkcaldy and Glasgow, with people buying and selling, how had people managed to behave in a coordinated and orderly way, with those things that people wanted most being made available?

As a young student at Glasgow, Smith still had the habit of talking to himself, which his friends found amusing and new acquaintances sometimes found annoying. In social circumstances he seemed shy and tended to stammer, and he was troubled with a nervous condition that caused his head to shake at times. He rode a horse well enough to get from one town to the next when necessary, but had little other daily physical exercise.

Adam worked hard for three years and excelled at his studies—especially mathematics, astronomy, and moral philosophy. A good writer, he expressed his well-thought-out opinions and beliefs clearly and in interesting ways. And although he stammered and stuttered in social settings, he was detailed and articulate when presenting formal speeches.

In 1740, seventeen-year-old Adam Smith's intelligence and hard work were recognized when he was awarded a Snell Exhibition—a prestigious scholarship made available to five Scotsmen to attend Oxford University and study for the ministry. Traveling by horseback, he left Glasgow for Oxford, England. The scholarship provided him with £40 a year to study at Balliol College, a constituent college of Oxford University, which had the reputation of being a superior institution for the study of religion, and there, following in the path of the Reverend Dr. Hutcheson, Smith could receive the education required to be ordained as a minister.

3 To Oxford and the Ministry

Adam Smith did not like Balliol College. He and the other four Snell Exhibitioner Scots were distinctly different from the other one hundred undergraduates at the college, in part because of their thick Scottish accents. Scots were not warmly welcomed at Oxford University—or anywhere in England for that matter. Smith discovered that anti-Unionism existed in England, just as it did in Scotland, with the English disliking the political union between England and Scotland about as much as the Scots did, but for different reasons. The Union of 1707 had forced the English to assume financial responsibilities for the Scots, including assuming the country's debts. Scotland lacked the infrastructure found in England, such as good roads for large carriages to transport mail, supplies, and passengers, and the English had to incur much of the expense for providing and maintaining this infrastructure.

Upon his arrival at Oxford University, Smith also discovered that serious religious and political differences existed between the two countries. Scottish lowlanders were predominantly Presbyterian and opposed Catholicism. At Balliol College, even though the official

A painting of the Battle of Killiecrankie, fought in 1689 between supporters of two rivals for the British throne. Highland Scots supported the deposed Catholic king, James VII, whereas Lowland Scots supported the Protestant William of Orange.

religion of England was the Protestant Church of England, Smith found administrative officials favored certain groups with Catholic sympathies, such as the Jacobites.

A person—Scottish or English—who supported King James VII was a Jacobite (the Latin word for James is Jacobus). For decades Scotland and England had shared a monarch but maintained separate parliaments. Because the countries supported different religious faiths, however, disagreements over religious practices had invoked constant political tensions that simmered between the two parliaments—tensions that had exploded when King James VII of Scotland, better known as King James II of England, converted from Protestantism to the Catholic faith of his wife. In the Glorious Revolution of 1688, the English parliament had deposed

King James for, among other things, his religious conversion. Several months later the Scottish parliament voted to do the same, which angered those Scots who supported King James. King James and his family fled to France. The first Jacobite rebellion occurred in 1689 when a few Scots attempted to restore the exiled king to the Scottish-English monarchy. The Jacobites did not succeed, as they failed to organize effectively.

Another Jacobite rebellion had occurred in 1708 when the exiled king's son, James VIII of Scotland (nicknamed the Old Pretender), a Catholic like his parents, attempted to take the throne of Great Britain by organizing a Scottish rebellion to attack England. The French king Louis XIV, who supported James's right to the throne, sponsored the rebellion. While lowlanders might not have been particularly loyal to England, they refused to join James's rebellion, in part because they feared the demise of the Presbytery Church if a Catholic king ruled Scotland. Only clans in the Catholic highlands were willing to take up the fight. Upon reaching Scotland, James and his army anchored off the Fife coast. They never made shore. Bad weather and the more powerful British Royal Navy thwarted James's plan to join the highland clans awaiting him.

Soon after the Union of 1707, a German had obtained the English-Scottish throne and was crowned King George I. By 1715, citizens of both Scotland and England were frustrated with the Union and King George I, who could not speak English.

Another Jacobite rebellion occurred in the northeast highlands in September 1715 when John Erskine, Earl of Mar, organized clans to attempt once again to place the Old Pretender James VIII of Scotland on the throne. Once again the lowlanders chose not to fight. They might not like being ruled by a German king but at least he supported a Protestant religion, which was more in line with the Presbytery Church than the Catholicism advocated by James. In this campaign the Jacobites greatly outnumbered King George's army. Yet the Jacobites lost in the battle of Sherriffmuir because of poor leadership.

Though James VIII had suffered defeat again, King George and Parliament began taking the Jacobite threat more seriously. From 1715 through 1740 more than 250 miles of expensive roads, bridges, and forts were built throughout Scotland to ensure the rapid deployment of troops in the event of another rebellion. It was money that some English students at Oxford University resented England having to pay.

Smith kept his opinions on religion and politics largely to himself, so his opinion on the Jacobites is unknown. But when Smith began his studies at Oxford in 1740, many English and Scottish lowlanders still detested Catholicism, even though they had become more tolerant of other religious faiths. Also, the English king (now King George II) and Parliament remained wary of the Jacobites and another possible uprising. Yet Smith discovered a core of Oxford University administrators who discriminated in favor of people known to have Jacobite sympathies, thus placing lowlander Smith on the wrong side because of his origin. Furthermore, he experienced ridicule by those at Oxford University who did not like the poor, unsophisticated Scotsman from the Presbytery lowlands.

In addition to political, religious and cultural differences, Smith encountered differences that had an even greater impact on his opinion of Balliol College. Smith could not find a professor he admired anywhere at Oxford. In Scotland students paid most of their professor's salary directly. If a professor did not teach well, students would not pay to attend the professor's class. At Oxford University the professors—or dons, as they were called—received a salary whether they taught well or not. Nor were there as many formal lectures offered at Balliol College as there had been at Glasgow. In a letter written in 1740 to his cousin and guardian William Smith (who worked for the Duke of Argyll, a powerful Scottish nobleman), he complained that no student

This eighteenth-century view of Broad Street in Oxford, England, shows several of the University of Oxford colleges. Smith attended Balliol College, which was founded in the late 1200s.

should ever fear endangering "his health at Oxford by excessive Study, our only business here being to go to prayers twice a day, and to lecture twice a week."

Years later Adam Smith would comment on the ineffectual teachers he encountered at Oxford University in his famous book *The Wealth of Nations*. Smith saw the problem in the way his professors were paid. He wrote, "The endowments of schools and colleges have necessarily diminished more or less the necessity of application in the teachers. Their subsistence, as far as it arrives from their salaries, is evidently derived from a fund altogether independent of their success and reputation in their par-

NICCOLÒ MACCHIAVELLI

ticular professions." He added, "In the University of Oxford, the greater part of the public professors have for these many years, given up altogether even the pretence of teaching." There was no one like Professor Hutcheson at Balliol College.

Smith found solace in the library, surrounded by books. Fortunately, there were even more great books to read in the library at Oxford University than at the University of Glasgow. Rather than attend lectures and study with the dons as he had done at Glasgow, Smith taught himself by reading an enormous number of books. For six years he dutifully used his scholarship money to pay tuition for classes he did not attend while learning on his own about the Roman and Greek classics, the arts, English literature, and science, especially astronomy. He read the great political philosophers, such as the sixteenth-century Italian philosopher, Machiavelli, and the books of the Italian astronomer and mathematician Galileo, who had been criticized and imprisoned by the Italian government and the church for writing about his scientific findings. Smith learned that reading, as well as writing, books could also get a person in trouble.

During his time at Oxford, Smith shunned lectures and did not study under the supervision of professors. Instead he read widely on his own. Among the thinkers he studied were the political philosopher Niccolo Machiavelli (opposite) and the mathematician and astronomer Galileo Galilei (above).

Smith had acquired a controversial book—*A Treatise of Human Nature*—written by Hutcheson's friend, David Hume. There were three volumes in total. The first two had been published in 1739 anonymously. The third had been published in 1740 under Hume's name. Hume—a known skeptic who questioned many traditional beliefs of the times, including certain religious beliefs—had received both wide public acclaim and criticism; especially criticism from the church, which still did not approve of people questioning the official church view on God and religion. Although never imprisoned for writing his book, the twenty-nine-year-old Hume was publicly berated by religious authorities in both England and Scotland as a heretic.

At Oxford, certain university administrators did not approve of Hume's views on God and religion either. Smith was caught with the book and punished. He received a harsh reprimand from a university official and the book was seized. As a lowly Scotsman on scholarship at Balliol College, Smith could not protest the loss of his property. He knew that Oxford University students had been expelled for lesser transgressions in the recent past. Freedom of speech and the freedom to read what one wanted were more restricted at Oxford than at the University of Glasgow.

Smith soon discovered another difference between the two countries and universities—loneliness. Smith had only two or three friends in England. Other than William Smith, who resided on occasion at the Duke of Argyll's estate in England, Smith did not have family close by and the distance of more than 350 miles between Oxford and Kirkcaldy made visits home too expensive.

As the years passed, Smith continued to spend hours alone studying in the library, although he confessed to being without discipline at writing personal letters. In a letter to his mother written November 29, 1743, he wrote, "I think of you every day, but always defer writing till the post is just going, and then sometimes business or company, but oftener laziness, hinders me."

Living in England had not improved Smith's frail health. Upon discovering tar water as a popular remedy for such diseases as scurvy and shaking of the head, he wrote to his mother expressing his wish that she try it too. Life at Oxford remained routine and largely solitary until 1745. Twenty-two-year-old Smith saw his routine interrupted when his homeland became involved in yet another Jacobite rebellion.

The final Jacobite uprising occurred in June 1745 when the son of James VIII, Prince Charles Edward Stuart (also known as Bonnie Prince Charlie), decided to invade Scotland and England and crown his father as king. Growing impatient with waiting for the French to support his efforts to invade Great Britain, twenty-three-year-old Charles ambitiously set sail on his own and organized support among the northeast highland clans to fight the English and those Scots loyal to the English monarchy of George II. Taking advantage of the Scottish roads and bridges financed by King George I, Prince Charles and his army captured Edinburgh and proceeded to march into England to recapture the crown.

First, however, he needed more money and men to succeed in his campaign. When King Louis XV of France finally sent money and a ship to support the rebellion, success appeared possible, until Scots loyal to the English government captured the ship. Undeterred, Charles marched to Derby in the south of England, but without reinforcements, he was overwhelmed by the British army and forced to retreat back into Scotland. Charles refused to give up even though he had few

In 1745, Bonnie Prince Charlie organized support among Scottish Highland clans to put his father, James VIII, on the British throne. This final Jacobite uprising was defeated in 1746.

supplies, little money, and a fatigued and unsettled army. On Christmas Day, the army reached Glasgow, where they remained for ten days before proceeding north to the highlands.

On April 16, 1746, the war ended at Culloden Moor, near the town of Inverness in the Highlands. Bonnie Prince Charlie hid in the highlands. By dressing as a woman he avoided capture and eventually escaped to France. Others left behind were not so lucky.

King George II showed little mercy for the Jacobites or anyone with Jacobite sympathies living in Scotland, especially those traitors in the highlands (although sympathizers at Oxford University were ignored). Jacobite highlanders were arrested, imprisoned, and sometimes executed. Scottish estates in the highlands were confiscated and the clan system partly dismantled. Plaid clothing and bagpipes were outlawed, along with other items representing traditional Highland culture.

In the lowlands, those Scots who did not want a pro-Catholic monarchy had cause to celebrate the end of the Jacobite rebellion. The monarchies of King George I and II had consistently shown toleration for the Presbytery Church, and with the threat of the Catholic James VIII ever ruling England and Scotland now seemingly dead, Protestantism was secured.

Also, for the lowlanders at least, the end of the Jacobite rebellion had secured the prosperity of Scotland. Over time more and more Scots had begun to realize that the Union of 1707 was good for their country. The Union had greatly improved economic conditions, especially in the lowlands. More trade with countries in the vast British Empire had caused parts of Scotland to progress rapidly. Glasgow had become a major port in the British Empire as a result of trade with British territories such as the American colonies. The Scots were getting wealthier. English taxes might be higher than the lowlanders were accustomed to paying, but the increased wealth accumulated by most individuals had greatly made up for the increase in taxes. Because of the Union, the Scottish infrastructure had improved significantly. The lowlanders had only to look at their new roads and bridges providing easier and faster transportation between cities to know they were better off in 1745 than before the Union of 1707.

Scotland might be better off, but life was still difficult for Smith living in England. For six years he had resided far away from home at Oxford University where scorn for unsophisticated Presbytery Scotsmen continued as it had for centuries. The Snell Exhibition covered ten years of study and students could request a one-year extension, which meant that Smith had four to five more years of solitary existence at Balliol College left. Furthermore, if he fulfilled the requirements of the Snell Exhibition, Smith would then become ordained not as a minister of the Presbytery Church, but of the Church of England.

In August 1746 at the age of twenty-three, Smith left Oxford and returned home to Kirkcaldy. He decided not to continue with his studies for the ministry. The decision must have been particularly difficult to make. It was not until February 4, 1749, that Smith wrote to the Reverend Dr. Theophilus Leigh, Master of Balliol and Vice-Chancellor of Oxford University (and a known Jacobite sympathizer), officially resigning his Snell Exhibition.

4 Scholarly Beginnings

About the same time that Adam Smith left Oxford University, Francis Hutcheson contracted a fever while visiting his family home in Dublin, Ireland, and died. For the next two years Smith had no job and no mentor. Living with his mother in Kirkcaldy, he continued reading and studying on his own until Henry Home, a Scottish judge in Edinburgh, encouraged Smith to give public lectures on rhetoric and belles lettres—the study of literature, especially creative or imaginative works.

Henry Home (who became known as Lord Kames in 1752) was a close friend of David Hume and Francis Hutcheson. Home also had been friends with a former resident of Kirkcaldy, James Oswald of Dunnikier, a longtime friend of the Smith family. Oswald's younger brother John Oswald and Smith had attended the Burgh School together. Oswald's father, also known as James, had helped Margaret take care of Adam Smith Sr.'s burial arrangements back in 1723. And the Oswald family had once owned a nail-making business that curious boys liked to visit, including Smith.

Henry Home, a Scottish judge who was close friends with David Hume and Francis Hutcheson, encouraged Smith to give a series of public lectures.

Smith followed up on Home's suggestion and began traveling between Kirkcaldy and Edinburgh in 1748 to present his series of public lectures. Each person paid the price of one guinea to attend a series. Approximately one hundred people attended Smith's inaugural series, making it a financial success.

In addition to the lectures on English literature, which were delivered for three successive winters, Smith presented at least one series on economics in the winter of 1750-1751. In this series, Smith advocated the doctrines of commercial liberty—a subject he had first learned about in the lectures of Dr. Hutcheson years before. Members of the literati were discussing and debating this subject as well. Three such men included Hume, Home, and Oswald, who were corresponding on economic issues; Home and Oswald also corresponded with Smith. James Oswald had served as commissioner of the navy since 1745, and he had the added responsibility of representing his Scottish burgh in the English parliament. Well known for his mastery of economics, he publicly sided with those members of the literati and politicians seeking changes to the mercantilist laws.

The Edinburgh lectures were not only popular, but impressed people with Smith's scholarship and intellectual insight. The lectures brought him enough critical esteem that influential university professors in both Edinburgh and Glasgow accepted Smith as a new member of the literati. At the same time, two important events occurred that significantly affected Smith's life.

First, Professor Loudon, who held the chair of logic at the University of Glasgow, died, giving Smith an opportunity to become a professor at a major Scottish university. He was unanimously elected to the chair of logic at the beginning of 1751, and on January 10, 1751, Smith wrote to the Clerk of Senate Robert Simson, professor of mathematics, accepting the prestigious university professorship. Following ceremonial procedures, Smith read the dissertation he had written, *De origine idearum*, before the faculty. Next he took the pledge of faithful administration—the oath of *De fideli*—before the university administrators. Once he had signed the Westminster Confession of Faith before the Presbytery of Glasgow, his new job as a professor of the University of Glasgow became official.

The second major event that occurred was the death of Smith's half brother, Hugh Smith. Upon the death of their father in 1723, the estate had been divided three ways with Margaret, Smith, and Hugh each receiving one-third. (James Oswald Sr. of Dunnikier—father to John and James—was appointed a trustee to both of the Smith children, although he died before fulfilling his responsibilities.) After his father's funeral, Hugh had moved away from Kirkcaldy to attend a boarding school somewhere in Scotland. Hugh had long suffered from frequent pulmonary ailments and when he died at age forty-one, unmarried and childless, he left no will. Adam Smith inherited Hugh's estate. Although Margaret received no money directly, Smith saw that she was well cared for. She even moved with him to Glasgow, along with a cousin, Janet Douglas, and the three lived in a house provided by the university. Janet assisted Margaret in supervising a servant or two and managing the household affairs.

Soon after Smith took the chair of logic position at the university, the chair of moral philosophy position became available when the holder of the chair, Professor Craigie, took ill and died. Smith was asked to assume the responsibilities for both chairs until a replacement could be hired. Fortunately, Smith was adequately prepared for the dual role. The public lecture series on belles lettres and economics that he had presented in Edinburgh could be used to teach the students of both logic and moral philosophy.

When it came time to hire a replacement, Smith decided to switch positions and he relinquished the chair of logic. On April 29, 1752, university authorities officially appointed Smith to the chair of moral philosophy—the same chair Francis Hutcheson had held. One candidate for the chair of logic was the controversial David Hume. Smith gave his opinion on the candidate, writing that "I should prefer David Hume to any man for a colleague; but I am afraid the public would not be of my opinion; and the interest of the society will oblige us to have some regard to the opinion of the public." Hume did not get the chair.

Following in the path of Professor Hutcheson, Smith taught philosophy, politics, and economics. He lectured on natural liberty—a person's natural desire for freedom to think and express his or her thoughts. He explained his belief that it was an individual's freedom to trade with anyone he or she wanted, including people who lived in other countries.

There were about three hundred students at the University of Glasgow. Of these three hundred students, Smith taught about eighty students in his public course. Each student paid one guinea and a half to attend the public course, which was required for graduation. Of these eighty students, he taught twenty in the private course. These students again paid one guinea each; many of them were preparing to be Presbyterian ministers and wanted to pursue the subject of moral philosophy in more depth.

The college session began in mid-October and ended in mid-June. Smith taught every weekday from seven-thirty to eight-thirty in the morning. At eleven he held a voluntary one-hour class to re-examine the contents of the earlier session. Twice a week he met with students attending the private course. And he made himself available to meet with students individually, or in small groups, just as Hutcheson had met with him. A popular lecturer, although not the dynamic speaker that Hutcheson had been, Smith was paid well by his students. His influence extended beyond the university. As a member of at least two clubs, the Literary Society and the Glasgow Economic Society, he presented papers on subjects such as jurisprudence and politics, including his views on free trade, in which he made a case for free trade among countries.

Smith took his administrative duties as seriously as his professorial ones. Even though Smith's keen ability to concentrate on a particular subject may have caused him to be distracted to the point of being absentminded on occasion, this did not deter him from having a good sense for the business of university administration. As part of his responsibilities, he served as a member of the faculty Senatus. He took care of university matters as simple as dealing with the holly hedge in the college's garden to traveling to Edinburgh on behalf of the university to handle important financial matters. During his travels to Edinburgh, he even served as a liaison between the Senatus of the University of Glasgow and Balliol College administrators in a matter regarding the Snell Exhibition scholarships.

Frequent trips to Edinburgh had an added benefit—he could visit friends. He saw Henry Home—now Lord Kames—and James Oswald. Increasingly, Smith began to spend time with David Hume and the two became close friends. Smith became a member of the Philosophical Society of Edinburgh, and in 1754 he helped found the celebrated Edinburgh Select Society.

The idea of such a society had come from another one of Smith's friends, the famous painter, Allan Ramsay. Modeled after societies popular in France, the Select Society served as a debating club for discussing topics of the day and as a means for promoting the arts, sciences, and manufacturers of Scotland. The Society grew quickly from fifteen to 130 members. In addition to

Smith's friends, members included prominent artists, scientists, professors, ministers, physicians, businessmen, bankers, and politicians. Important guests attended meetings, such as the British politician Charles Townshend. The Society became famous for its organized and enthusiastic debates, covering topics ranging from religion to economics. An example was whether bounties on the export of corn would be advantageous to manufacturing as well as to agriculture.

A self-portrait of Allan Ramsay. The Scottish painter wanted to start an intellectual society like those popular in France. The result was the Edinburgh Select Society, of which Ramsay's friend Adam Smith was one of fifteen founding members.

All subject areas were encouraged for debate with one exception: any topic that might conjure further Jacobite strife was forbidden, such as the question of whether Scotland should be entitled to have its own militia. (England had prohibited the Scots from having their own militia as a result of the 1745 Jacobite rebellion.)

Although the Society openly debated religiously sensitive topics, such as whether tolerance to a variety of protestant religious beliefs would benefit Britain, without encountering any apparent repercussions from the Presbytery Church, this did not mean that the Church's stormy relationship with certain Select Society members had changed, especially David Hume. His contention with the Church continued to get Hume into trouble. In a letter written to Smith dated March 1757, Hume wrote: "Did you ever hear of such Madness and Folly as our Clergy have lately fallen into? For my Part, I expect that the next Assembly will very solemnly pronounce the Sentence of Excommunication against me: But I do not apprehend it to be a Matter of any Consequence. What do you think?" A threat of excommunication did occur, although it was not carried out. Undeterred, Hume continued to write on topics that upset the Church.

Besides his university and society activities, Smith spent much time attending the theater in both Glasgow and Edinburgh, an interest he shared with his friend Hume. The theater was undergoing a complete transformation in the mid-1700s. Where it had once been a crude facility with a covered stage for the actors and an open outdoor arrangement for the audience (which made scheduling plays subject to weather conditions), expensive ornate playhouses were designed by prominent architects. Inside the new playhouse theaters one could hear the orchestra playing the music of popular composers like Handel and Gluck. One could observe operatic singers and actors, such as the famous English actress Peg Woffington, performing on stage in their elaborate costumes and exotic makeup. To set the proper scene, well-known painters were employed to create the magnificent backdrops. In the new theater design, there was need for an engineer, who, without ever being seen by the audience, operated the ropes and pulleys that helped manipulate the giant sets and trigger the added stage effects.

This eighteenth-century illustration shows an audience, wearing fashionable wigs, at a theater show. Smith was an avid fan of the theater, attending performances in Glasgow and Edinburgh.

Smith had personal affairs that kept him busy as well. He became romantically attached to a beautiful and accomplished Scottish lady, although the two never married. He also regularly involved himself in assisting relatives and friends to obtain suitable positions and higher-salaried jobs. In a letter written to Lord of Admiralty Mr. Gilbert Elliot, a friend of Hume's, Smith sought to assist a relative by marriage, John Currie, by recommending him for a job. As Smith explained, Currie "has had the imprudence to make a love marriage with a young Lady, a cousin of mine for whom I have always had a very high regard, but who had not a single shilling to her fortune."

Throughout his active years at Glasgow, Smith's reputation as a great teacher began to grow through his dedication to teaching and educating his students. He fulfilled his duties as a member of the Senatus, made new friends among the faculty, including Joseph Black, the lecturer in chemistry, and maintained strong relationships with his many old friends, all the while staying actively engaged with his clubs and literary societies in Glasgow and Edinburgh. And between 1758 and 1764 Smith managed the library funds.

He became involved in helping a future scholar. Upon receiving a letter requesting that he take a boarder, Mr. Fitzmaurice, into his home to direct the young man's education at the University of Glasgow, Smith agreed. In exchange Smith was to be paid at least £100 a year. Always conscientious in fulfilling his duties, Smith corresponded with the boy's father, Lord Shelburne, to report on his son's progress. Smith wrote on February 21, 1759, that "Fitzmaurice attends all his classes with the most exact punctuality and gives more application to his studies than could reasonably be expected. I find him perfectly tractable and docile in every respect and I heartily wish that we may give the same satisfaction to him which he gives to all of us." Smith wrote again to Lord Shelburne a month later commending Fitzmaurice on his punctuality and attendance to classes. "He attends different Masters for Greek, Latin and Philosophy five hours a day, and is besides employ'd with me at home between two and three hours, in going over the subjects of those different lectures. He reads too every day some thing by himself and a good deal on Saturdays and Sundays when he has most leisure."

Smith found time in his busy schedule to write on astronomy and philosophy. In 1759 Smith's first book, *The Theory of Moral Sentiments*, was published. Before this time he had only one other published work, a book review published in 1755 in the *Edinburgh Review* of Samuel Johnson's *Dictionary of the English Language*.

Chemist Joseph Black, a colleague and friend of Smith's at the University of Glasgow, is credited with discovering carbon dioxide.

Immediately after its publication, Smith began revising his book to correct some grammatical mistakes. He also continued his work on a history of the astronomical systems up to René Descartes, a French philosopher, mathematician, and scientist. With his days productive and full, with friends and family surrounding him and a career that he loved, life was good for Adam Smith.

5 The Theory of Moral Sentiments

The Theory of Moral Sentiments was not considered a book about economics when it was published. Indeed, Smith was not thought of as an economist in 1759 since there was no separate academic field of study known as economics at the time. He was a professor of moral philosophy, and moral philosophy covered a broad field of subjects involving how people should and do behave. Smith wrote *The Theory of Moral Sentiments* to explain how people manage to control their emotions and desires so they sympathize with others and deal with one another peacefully and productively. In other words, Smith was interested in how and why people cooperate.

Even though economics was not a separate field of study in 1759, the literati wrote about economic topics, and Smith devoted much of his lectures to those issues. Although *The Theory of Moral Sentiments* may not have been initially thought of as a book about economics, in important ways it was about the very foundation of a prosperous economy. Producing wealth requires that people cooperate by pursuing their own advantages in ways that benefit others. People have to be willing to coordinate their efforts in cooperation with others, so that they can produce the goods and services that others want. Furthermore, every individual has to depend on others to coordinate their efforts to produce the goods and services that he wants. And, ideally, this cooperation would result from a widespread willingness to treat each other fairly, honestly, and sympathetically. Smith argued in *The Theory of Moral Sentiments* that such willing cooperation is possible, and that individual liberty is compatible with economic prosperity.

Smith did not originate the idea that cooperation is important to economic prosperity. Members of the literati, such as the English political philosopher, Thomas Hobbes, had

THE

THEORY

OF

MORAL SENTIMENTS.

By ADAM SMITH,
PROFESSOR of MORAL PHILOSOPHY in the
University of GLASGOW.

LONDON:
Printed for A. MILLAR, in the STRAND;
And A. KINCAID and J. BELL, in EDINBURGH.
MDCCLIX.

The title page to Smith's first book,
The Theory of Moral Sentiments.

written about it in the seventeenth century. But Smith approached the idea from a different angle, and he opposed the commonly accepted view of Hobbes that people were basically selfish, and, therefore, cooperation was impossible if people were free to pursue their own interests. This Hobbesian view had also been rejected by Hutcheson, in his lectures that Smith attended.

As mentioned previously, Hobbes had argued that if people were free to make their own decisions, their selfish impulses would destroy any hope for productive cooperation and result in life being "nasty, brutish, and short." Hobbes argued that the only way to get people to treat each other with decency and to work together for the common good was by giving a powerful government (the king or queen and their officials) almost unlimited authority to make people behave in ways they would never choose on their own.

English political philosopher Thomas Hobbes believed that only by submitting to the authority of an absolute ruler could human beings overcome their innate selfishness and cooperate meaningfully with one another. Adam Smith disagreed with this view.

Smith, too, recognized the important role of government in maintaining an orderly society, but he thought government's role should be far more limited than did Hobbes. He rejected "so odious a doctrine" of extensive government control over our lives advocated by Hobbes and others who had little faith in human liberty. *In The Theory of Moral*

Sentiments, Smith applauded "The disposition to the affections which tend to unite men in society, to humanity, kindness, natural affection, friendship, esteem," even if these affections "may sometimes be excessive." He summed up his view that free people were capable of behaving with decency toward others when he stated near the end of his book, "the mind was naturally endowed with a faculty, by which it distinguished in certain actions and affections, the qualities of right, laudable, and virtuous, and in others those of wrong, blamable, and vicious."

Smith was not naïve about human nature. He recognized that people have a strong regard for their own interests and are not always happy with the success of others. He pointed out, for example, that we often express happiness in the good fortune of our neighbors, "when in our hearts, perhaps, we are really sorry." He also understood that the appetites and passions activated by self-interest could lead to harmful outcomes, unless directed in desirable ways by social institutions, and moderated by more noble impulses. The esteemed Irish lawyer, writer, and British politician, Edmund Burke, expressed Smith's concerns about the connection between liberty and control over our self-interest in the well-known statement:

> Men are qualified for civil liberty in exact proportion to their disposition to put chains on their own appetites. . . . Society cannot exist unless a controlling power upon will and appetite be placed somewhere, and the less of it there is within, the more there must be without. It is ordained in the eternal constitution of things, that men of intemperate minds cannot be free. Their passions forge their fetters.

British writer and statesman Edmund Burke (center) at a literary party in London. Burke praised Smith's *The Theory of Moral Sentiments* for its originality.

But while Smith recognized the danger of too much self-interest, he rejected Hobbes' extremely negative view of human nature for three reasons. First, he believed that up to some point self-interest was a benevolent gift of nature. Smith wrote that "Every man is, no doubt, by nature, first and principally recommended to his own care; and as he is fitter to take care of himself than of any other person, it is fit and right that it should be so." Second, Smith believed that a beneficial social order could emerge from the pursuit of self-interest when directed by proper social institutions and rules. Third, Smith believed that, with few exceptions, people were not inherently evil. He thought that people were motivated by more noble sentiments than just self-interest, such as sympathy with and concern for others, and in *The Theory of Moral Sentiments* he set out to explain why.

What would become one of the best-known sentences in *The Theory of Moral Sentiments* was the first sentence, in which Smith wrote, "How selfish soever man may be supposed, there are evidently some principles in his nature, which interest him in the fortune of others, and render their happiness necessary to him, though he derives nothing from it except the pleasure of seeing it. . . . The greatest ruffian, the most hardened violator of the laws of society, is not altogether without [concern for the well-being of others]."

Smith's explanation of why people have a strong tendency to consider the interests of others was based on the universal desire to be popular and respected. He believed that the desire for popularity and respect was stronger even than the desire for the things that money can buy. Smith wrote, "The desire of becoming the proper objects of this respect [respect from others], of deserving and obtaining this credit and rank among our equals, is, perhaps, the strongest of all our desires, and our anxiety to obtain the advantages of fortune is accordingly much more excited and irritated by this desire, than by that of supplying all the necessities and conveniences of the body, which are always very easily supplied."

Because Smith knew that neither a man nor a woman could know for certain how others felt about his or her behavior, he argued that "As we have no immediate experience of what other men feel, we can form no idea of the manner in which they are affected, but by conceiving what we ourselves should feel in the like situation." But, each individual must have help in his effort to judge how others respond to certain behavior. This help, he concluded, came in the form of the impartial spectator—a type of conscience that tells us, as honestly as possible, the effect of our actions on others and how others are actually responding to us. As Smith pointed out, "It is so disagreeable to think ill of ourselves, that we often purposely turn away our view from those circumstances which might render that judgment unfavourable." Smith believed it is a man's desire for the favorable opinion of others, and his ability to modify his behavior in response to what he sees as admirable behavior in others, that develop a man's moral sense.

Dugald Stewart, whose father and Smith knew one another as students at the University of Glasgow, summed up Smith's moral theory in a formal paper presented to the Royal Society of Edinburgh in 1793. He wrote that "The fundamental principle of Mr. Smith's theory is, that the primary objects of our moral perceptions are the actions of other men; and that our moral judgments with respect to our own conduct are only applications to ourselves of decisions which we have already passed on the conduct of our neighbour." Or in Smith's words, "The principle by which we naturally either approve or disapprove of our own conduct, seems to be altogether the same with that by which we exercise the like judgments concerning the conduct of other people."

Contrary to commonly held views in 1759, Smith believed that a person's moral judgments were sincere, and that they went deeper than superficial appearances motivated by the desire to be popular—people have moral sentiments for reasons that go beyond a calculation of self-interest. In his book, he disagreed with those who, according to him, "are fond of deducing all our sentiments from certain refinements of self-love . . ." Smith wrote that:

> Man naturally desires, not only to be loved, but to be lovely; or to be that thing which is the natural and proper object of love. He naturally dreads, not only to be hated, but to be hateful; or to be that thing which is the natural and proper object of hatred. He desires, not only praise, but praiseworthiness; or to be that thing which, though it should be praised by nobody, is, however, the natural and proper object of praise. He dreads, not only blame, but blameworthiness; or to be that thing which, though it should be blamed by nobody, is, however, the natural and proper object of blame.

Smith rejected the arguments of those who believed that a person treated others nicely only to get something in return:

> When we have read a book or poem so often that we can no longer find any amusement in reading it by ourselves, we still take pleasure in reading it to a companion. To him it has all the graces of novelty; we enter into the surprise and admiration which it naturally excites in him, but which it is no longer capable of exciting in us; we consider all the ideas which it presents rather in the light in which they appear to him, than in that in which they appear to ourselves, and we are amused by sympathy with his amusement which thus enlivens our own.

And yet, Smith was not reluctant to point out that even though virtue may be its own reward, there are other rewards as well. He continued that "No benevolent man ever lost altogether the fruits of his benevolence. If he does not always gather them from the persons from whom he ought to have gathered them, he seldom fails to gather them, and with a tenfold increase, from other people."

In *The Theory of Moral Sentiments*, therefore, Smith sought to show that self-interest was not as dominant in human nature as commonly believed, and that the self-interest that did exist was desirable as long as it was directed by general rules. He believed that a large measure of liberty was consistent with a cooperative and prosperous social order.

Adam Smith's popularity as a teacher and a scholar greatly expanded after the publication of *The Theory of Moral Sentiments*. The acclaim he received in Scotland and England was soon matched by admiration and interest in his book by people outside Britain. Visiting dignitaries, such as the Americans Benjamin Franklin and his son, traveled to Scotland to meet Smith. Dr. Tronchin, a renowned physician in Geneva, Switzerland (and a friend of the famous Voltaire), sent his son to the University of Glasgow to study with Adam Smith. Students came from as far away as Russia to study with the celebrated thirty-six-year-old professor.

Hume sent Edmund Burke a copy of *The Theory of Moral Sentiments* soon after it was published, and Burke was so impressed that he wrote a glowing review in *The Annual Register*, especially praising the book for its originality. Burke then followed up with a letter to Smith, further complimenting his great work.

Hume wrote Smith congratulating him on the book and informing him that the British politician Charles Townshend, "the cleverest Fellow in England," hoped to entice Smith into resigning his professorship at the University of Glasgow to travel through Europe as the personal tutor to Townshend's stepson, the Duke of Buccleuch. Believing that Smith would never leave his esteemed position under any terms to travel and tutor the duke, Hume promised to visit Townshend and convince him to send the young nobleman to study with Smith at Glasgow instead.

Benjamin Franklin visited Smith in Edinburgh in 1759. By that time *The Theory of Moral Sentiments* had won Smith international acclaim as a scholar.

From 1759 through 1762 Smith continued to teach classes, travel on university business, visit friends, attend concerts and plays, and clubs and society meetings. From 1760 to 1762 he served as dean of faculty at the University of Glasgow. In recognition of his outstanding achievements as a professor at the University of Glasgow, he was awarded the honorary title of LL.D. (Doctor of Laws) and became recognized as Dr. Smith among his colleagues.

Smith helped found another club in 1762—the Edinburgh Poker Club. Its membership included most of the men in the Select Society. The purpose of the club was not playing cards, but to poke at or stir up opinion on a question that had the Scottish greatly agitated: whether Scotland should establish its own militia. The club was formed as a result of a bill introduced into the English parliament by two of Smith's friends, James Oswald and Gilbert Elliot. The English in Parliament, fearing another Jacobite rebellion should the Scots have their own army, failed to pass the bill. Scotland was incensed with this inequality of rights. If the English had a national defense, then the Scots rightly deserved their own defense, too. After all, the Scots had their national heritage to protect, an honor they believed that the English constantly tried to erase. Also, the Scots believed themselves vulnerable to attack from a foreign country because the English army was primarily engaged in protecting the borders of England, leaving the Scots almost defenseless. The members of the club

Armed Scottish Highlanders sit around a campfire. Smith helped found the Edinburgh Poker Club in 1762 to address whether Scotland should have the right to establish its own militia.

were more talk than action, however, and slowly it faded away.

Being busy in his many professional and social pursuits did not keep Smith from his writing. While the publication of *The Theory of Moral Sentiments* and subsequent recognition established his reputation as a highly respected moral philosopher and a leading member of the literati, Smith had already begun shifting his interest more toward politics and economic issues, and the type of institutions and laws that promoted prosperity in a free society.

Although hailed by critics as a great book on moral philosophy, in many respects *The Theory of Moral Sentiments* was about economics—about how people can work together in ways that make them more productive. After years of watching men and women in the ports of Kirkcaldy and Glasgow buy and sell goods, listening to Hutcheson's lectures on law and economics, and talking to manufacturers such as his childhood friend, James Oswald, Smith had developed a keen interest in how people who are in direct, or fairly close, contact can cooperate. But the harmonious interaction Smith observed in one port or town was part of a larger pattern of harmonious interaction that took place between people dispersed all over the world. By shifting his interest to topics that were naturally viewed as economic, such as international trade, Smith began pondering how the range of cooperation considered in *The Theory of Moral Sentiments* could be expanded.

This shift of interest was explained by Dugald Stewart in his formal presentation to the Royal Society of Edinburgh; he said that after the publication of *The Theory of Moral Sentiments* "the plan of his [Smith's] lectures underwent a considerable change. His ethical doctrines, of which he had now published so valuable a part, occupied a much smaller portion of the course than formerly; and accordingly, his attention was naturally directed to a more complete illustration of the principles of Jurisprudence and of Political Economy." Stewart further explained Smith's transition from morals to political economics when he continued with "It is probable, that the uninterrupted friendship he had always maintained with his old companion Mr. Oswald, had some tendency to encourage him in prosecuting this branch of his studies; and the publication of Mr. Hume's *Political Discourses* in the year 1752, could not fail to confirm him in those liberal views of commercial policy which had already opened to him in the course of his own inquiries."

In August 1763, Smith received a letter from Hume with good news. Hume had received an invitation to serve as secretary to the English Embassy in Paris, and he had accepted the position. He explained that he was hurried in his preparations to move, but that he "could not depart without bidding you Adieu." He concluded his letter by writing that he hoped it would be possible for the two of them to meet abroad. Adam Smith's life was about to change also, and a meeting between Smith and Hume in Paris would come much sooner than either one imagined.

6 Travels Abroad

In the autumn of 1763, Smith's satisfaction with his job as a professor at the University of Glasgow was affected by the offer he'd received from Charles Townshend—"cleverest Fellow in England"—to tutor his stepson, the Duke of Buccleugh. Hume had told Smith that Townsend would make the offer in 1759 after the publication of *The Theory of Moral Sentiments*, but he'd assumed Smith wouldn't be interested.

Townshend was at this time a minor politician in the English parliament who had married a woman of the nobility with children. In a letter written October 25, 1763, Charles Townshend officially offered Smith the position of traveling tutor to his stepson, the Duke of Buccleugh. Once the duke completed the winter term at Eton—the historically prestigious private boys school of the English nobility—he would be available to travel to continental Europe in Smith's company. Townshend believed that the eighteen-year-old boy would get a broader and better education by traveling through Europe with the distinguished professor Adam Smith than by attending a university. Given Smith's experience at Oxford, he had to agree—at least regarding a

The British statesman Charles Townshend (1725–1767) hired Smith to tutor his stepson. As a politician, Townshend is best known for a program of taxes levied on the American colonies that he proposed in 1767. The colonists strongly resisted the so-called Townshend Acts; the controversial taxes were one of many factors contributing to the Americans' ultimate decision to break away from Great Britain.

university education in England. The offer meant that at the age of forty-one Smith could change careers, and travel to countries such as France and Switzerland, meeting distinguished European literati he had corresponded with or read about. Smith would be paid a salary of around £300 per year plus expenses, considerably more than he was making as a professor. Most importantly, he would receive a lifetime pension of £300 a year—enough for Smith and his mother to be financially secure for the rest of their lives. Smith accepted the offer.

Soon after making his momentous decision, Smith received a letter from Hume, who was pleased to report that he had so far been treated much better in France than in his home country of Scotland. He described the many compliments on his philosophy and history books he had received from dukes, courtiers of the royal French court, and foreign ambassadors in both Paris and Fontainebleau.

Smith waited until December to respond to Hume's letter, telling him that he had received and accepted

Townshend's offer. As Hume had hoped, in a few short months the two friends could meet with one another in France. One issue still to be resolved, however, was where Smith's mother and cousin would live once he resigned from the University of Glasgow, which provided them a house. In January 1764 he was notified by his friend and colleague Joseph Black that the two women would be allowed to remain in the house for awhile, most likely through the spring. Then, before departing the university, Smith had one final duty to perform. He met with his students to return their tuition fees because he could not complete the term. The students at first refused to accept the money, but Smith insisted.

Smith and his new student, the duke, met in London at the end of January 1764. They traveled to Paris for a brief stay, visiting with Hume, then found permanent accommodations in the French city of Toulouse.

Just a few months after moving to the popular resort city, Smith was bored. The recommendations and letters of introduction Townshend had promised to send so that Smith and the duke could

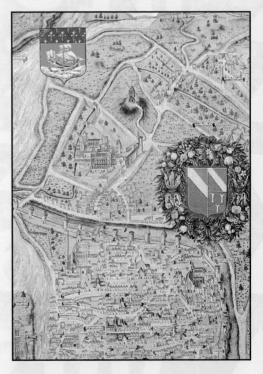

Paris was the most densely populated city in Europe when Smith visited with his Student, Henry Scott, 3rd Duke of Buccleugh.

meet new people had not materialized. Nor did it help that Smith could speak only a little French, and with his Scottish accent he spoke it badly. Although he had made a few new acquaintances, he found himself generally idle with nothing much of interest to keep him occupied. He wrote Hume asking his old friend to send a letter of recommendation to the Duke of Richelieu on Smith's behalf so that the two men could be officially introduced. At the end of the letter Smith admitted that life at Glasgow had been pleasurable and self-indulgent in comparison to the life he was living in France, and then he added, "I have begun to write a book in order to pass away the time. You may believe I have very little to do." The book he referred to would become *An Inquiry into the Nature and Causes of the Wealth of Nations*.

Smith and the duke had lived for seven months in Toulouse when they were joined by the duke's seven-

A nineteenth-century view of Toulouse, France. At Toulouse, Smith began work on what would become *An Inquiry into the Nature and Causes of the Wealth of Nations*.

teen-year-old younger brother, the Honorable Hew Campbell Scott. The three men lived and studied in Toulouse until the summer of 1765 when they left to tour the south of France. By fall they were in Switzerland. Dr. Tronchin, who had sent his son to study with Smith at the University of Glasgow, lived on the French-Swiss border near Geneva. So, too, did Tronchin's friend, the famous French author Francois Marie Arouet, otherwise known as Voltaire.

Born in 1694, Voltaire was a major figure in the Enlightenment, and had lived in Switzerland since 1755. The seventy-one-year-old poet, novelist, social philosopher, and playwright was widely respected for his many accomplishments, including his famous novel, *Candide*. A man of stormy temperament and an emotional show-off, Voltaire had once been imprisoned in the Bastille of France, risked his life quarreling with the king of Prussia, and made himself unwelcome in his native country by speaking openly against the French government and Catholic Church, before finding a permanent home in the more tolerant country of Switzerland.

In addition to Tronchin and Voltaire, Smith also met Marie-Louise Denis, Voltaire's niece and mistress. Smith thought Voltaire a great intellectual, and he and his two pupils remained in Switzerland for two months before returning to Paris to live, where they once again met up with Hume in December 1765.

In the famous social gatherings held in private homes—known as salons—French aristocrats discussed and debated subjects currently in vogue, which covered

Voltaire, a renowned novelist and social philosopher, was a major figure in the Enlightenment.

literature, metaphysics, theology, and philosophy. Hume, at least in Paris, was considered a king among the philosophers. Knowing Hume and having written a critically acclaimed book himself allowed Smith an easy introduction into the Parisian intellectual society. His French had improved as well. He often was invited to the salons, which were similar in purpose to the clubs and societies he frequented in Scotland, with the exception that notable French women not only attended, but often hosted (some competing with one another for famous guests) the gatherings of society's elite. Smith socialized regularly with such famous salon hostesses as Mademoiselle Rianecourt and the Comtesse de Boufflers. The former actress, Madame Riccoboni, who had given up the stage to become a novelist, was much impressed with Smith, the "philosopher of Glasgow," as he came to be known.

In the company of his new friends, Smith attended plays and enjoyed going to the opera. He also spent time with the distinguished French economists A. R. J. Turgot and Dr. Francois Quesnay (who also served as the king's personal physician), discussing, debating, and exchanging ideas on political economy systems, including what governments needed to do to make their subjects better off and their nations wealthy.

In both Switzerland and France, Smith observed governments in transition. Speaking to Tronchin and Voltaire, he learned of the difficulties the Swiss government had in maintaining significance in comparison to larger countries (In terms of population, Switzerland was one of the smallest countries in Europe.) At the time of Smith's visit, a struggle was underway between the two hundred families of privilege who had governed the small country for years and the citizens who, with encouragement and support from Voltaire, wanted a change from the traditional aristocratic government to a democratic republic. France had its problems, too. When visiting Turgot in Paris, or Quesnay at his apartment at the palace of Versailles, Smith had learned about the dissatisfaction growing among ordinary French people with the king and his court, a dissatisfaction that would lead to the French Revolution later in the century.

A painting of a French salon. Smith was often invited to participate in salon gatherings during his stay in France.

The situation in the American colonies and the Americans' growing dissatisfaction with the English government was also a topic of discussion in the salons of Paris during Smith's visit. The English parliament had begun imposing laws on the Americans that reduced freedoms they had previously taken for granted. First, the Sugar Act was passed to help pay off the debts England incurred in the French and Indian War. This Act increased the taxes paid for basic goods such as sugar and coffee imported into the thirteen colonies. The Act also forbade foreign alcohol, such as French wines, from being imported. Second, the English parliament made changes to the customs system, to help enforce the existing British trade laws that had been generally ignored in the American colonies. Third, Parliament passed the Currency Act, which prohibited the Americans from producing and issuing their own paper money. The American colonists were outraged. They complained of English taxation without parlia-

Bostonians protest the Stamp Act of 1765. Smith was sympathetic to the grievances of the American colonists and believed Britain should grant them more autonomy.

mentary representation, and in August 1764 a boycott of British goods had begun in Boston.

The English parliament squeezed tighter by passing the Quartering Act in March 1765—which required the Americans to supply housing and food for British troops—and the Stamp Act. The Stamp Act taxed printed materials: newspapers, pamphlets, bills, legal documents, licenses, almanacs, dice, and even playing cards. The tax was imposed on Americans to help pay for the costs of organizing and increasing a British military presence in America. At least with previous taxes, the money paid by the Americans for imported goods had flowed through the local legislatures of the thirteen colonies and then to England. For the first time, as part of the provision of the Stamp Act, the local legislatures were bypassed. Now the tax money was sent directly to England. Angry Americans began to organize resistance movements. By July 1765, as Smith and his pupils toured the south of France and Switzerland, organizations such as the Sons of Liberty had begun to take root in a number of American towns.

During his travels through Europe with Townshend's two sons, Smith spent hours talking to people, gaining knowledge, and proposing his beliefs and theories to many different people, including the ability of an economy based on private property and free exchange, with a limited government role, to create widespread opportunity and prosperity. He became increasingly convinced that most governments were pursuing economic policies that reduced the wealth of their economies and their citizens.

Smith believed that government was important. While he believed in an economic system based on free trade, in place of the mercantilist system, he believed that government should collect moderate taxes on goods shipped into the country (imports)—such as French wine—and goods shipped out of Great Britain (exports), such as Scottish nails. The question in Smith's opinion was not whether government should collect taxes, but how best to collect taxes, and the amount of taxes to collect that would be fair. After all, government needed revenues to serve the people by building schools, common roads, and bridges. The government also needed money to build a strong military to protect its citizens, rather than having countries within the British Empire waste resources to support their own militia—like Scotland wanted to do. Smith believed that the purpose of government was to be the servant of the people; it was not right to make people servants of the government. He had only to look at the great differences between the aristocrats with their government privileges and ordinary people, in every city he visited, to know that government needed to make some changes.

While Smith was touring Europe, people were beginning to speculate that America would eventually declare its independence from Great Britain. Smith was afraid that such a declaration would cause a war. Smith did not want a war between the American colonies and Great Britain. As opposed to what many people thought, Smith believed that war was not good for the economy. A good economy produced wealth and offered people opportunities to thrive. Wars destroyed wealth and killed people. Unless a country was defending itself, he believed that war should be avoided. Yet, he was sympathetic to American grievances, and believed that the American colonies should form a union with England, which would give them more autonomy over their affairs. As he discussed current events and ideas on economics and government policies with his many intellectual friends in Europe, his book (that he'd begun work on in Toulouse out of boredom) on how a country becomes wealthy began to take shape.

Smith lost one of his best-informed and closest friends, however, when Hume left France. Because of the ever-changing politics back in England, Hume was forced to leave his position at the English Embassy in January of 1766. He decided to move to England temporarily, while contemplating whether he should eventually return to Paris and make his home there indefinitely. (Smith counseled Hume to reside in Scotland and visit Paris.) Even though Hume may have been disappointed at having to leave a city where he and his ideas were enthusiastically accepted, he was not upset with the loss of the Embassy position. With his departure, he had managed to obtain a pension of £400 a year. "I have now Opulence and Liberty," Hume wrote to Smith.

Hume's life also was complicated by his friendship with Jean-Jacques Rousseau. Both famous and infamous, Rousseau had spent much of his fifty-four years stirring up controversy. In 1750 he had written in his *Discourse on the Sciences and Arts* that man's morality and virtue had been corrupted by the progress of the sciences and

Jean-Jacques Rousseau, an influential but controversial philosopher, fled France after the authorities issued a warrant for his arrest. In England, Adam Smith's friend David Hume came to Rousseau's aid—only to have Rousseau turn against him.

arts. His critical essays on political economy, society, and education had widespread influence throughout England and Europe, especially among French intellectuals. Angered by some of the things Rousseau had said, authorities attempted to suppress his writings, and he was constantly on the move in France and Switzerland to avoid having sanctions imposed on him. Life on the run soon became very uncomfortable, if not dangerous, for Rousseau. Much like Hume, Rousseau was despised by some and idolized by others. Hume befriended the controversial Rousseau—who many believed was emotionally unstable—and invited him to live in England.

Once the two were in London, Hume decided to help Rousseau reside in England under more permanent arrangements so that he could continue to write without interruption. After first obtaining Rousseau's permission, Hume successfully solicited a pension from King George III of England with which to support Rousseau and his writing endeavors indefinitely. The capricious Rousseau then publicly refused the pension, embarrassing the English court, yet making him a hero to certain members of the English literati.

Hume, frustrated and upset, spoke of openly exposing Rousseau for his ungrateful and callous behavior by writing and publishing an account of his actions. Smith wrote Hume from Paris in July 1766, arguing against a public battle between two illustrious members of the literati. "By endeavouring to unmask before the Public this hypocritical Pedant, you run the risk, of disturbing the tranquility of your whole life." Smith argued that Rousseau was using Hume for purposes of notoriety and that his friends in Paris agreed that he should not fight and criticize Rousseau publicly. Feeling compelled to defend himself, Hume published a pamphlet anyway.

In August, Smith had another worry to concern him. The duke, after falling from his horse while hunting, became ill. Smith immediately wrote Townshend a long letter explaining that the duke had developed a slight fever. He provided minute details of the patient's condition, such as "He vomited, but not enough to relieve him. I found his pulse extremely quick; he went to bed immediately and drank some vinegar whey." Smith assured Townshend that he had personally sat with the duke from early in the morning until late at night. The next day Smith sent for his friend Dr. Quesnay, personal physician to the king of France, who, himself feeling ill, turned the treatment of the duke over to the queen's physician, De la Saone. De la Saone decided that the fever was not violent enough to require bleeding from leeches attached to the skin, and continued to monitor the young man's condition for several days until the fever cleared.

Six weeks later Smith had reason to contact the duke's family again when nineteen-year-old Hew Campbell Scott became ill with a fever. Smith wrote to the boy's sister, Lady Frances Scott, describing in detail her brother's symptoms and condition. When Hew's condition did not improve quickly, Smith called in several physicians for assistance, including Dr. Tronchin and Dr. Quesnay. Smith assured Lady Frances in another letter written October 15 of the young man's excellent care, and that as Hew's symptoms had improved, the physicians' hopes were high for her brother's recovery. Sadly, though, Hew died on October 19, 1766. Smith and the duke returned to England in November with the body.

For six months, Smith remained in London. At the age of forty-three he had not lost his reputation for being absentminded. Being visited one morning by a distinguished gentleman, Smith, while lecturing like a professor, placed a piece of buttered bread into a teapot and poured water over it. When Smith finally paused long enough to take a sip of tea, he declared his drink the worst tea he had ever tasted.

He stayed busy in London. He was elected Fellow of the Royal Society, met with his publisher and saw the third revision of *The Theory of Moral Sentiments* published in 1767. He also counseled Townshend, who sought Smith's advice on economics. Townshend had recently been appointed to the important position of chancellor of the exchequer for Great Britain. As the man in charge of budgets and taxes for the crown, Townshend wanted more money from the American colonists and in his new position was actively engaged in convincing Parliament to pass several new tax laws.

The Duke of Buccleuch married in May, ending Smith's job as a traveling tutor. Even though the tutoring position had been terminated prematurely, the duke insisted on Smith receiving his pension, for life. His teaching career and tutoring travels now completed, Smith returned to Kirkcaldy to live with his mother and Janet and to continue writing his book, *An Inquiry into the Nature and Causes of the Wealth of Nations.*

7 from Kirkcaldy to London

or the next six years Smith worked full time, writing from his home in Kirkcaldy. He frequently took breaks by strolling along the bay. He resumed his habit of observing the hustle and bustle of active business around the port. He also met with longtime friends, such as James Oswald. But writing was Smith's primary activity.

There was his *The Theory of Moral Sentiments* to revise for the fourth time, and his *An Inquiry into the Nature and Causes of the Wealth of Nations* (or *The Wealth of Nations* for short), begun years earlier while living in Toulouse with the duke, was growing into a major project. Pacing the floor in his home—at times pausing to rub his head against the wall—Smith, who had a reputation for poor penmanship, dictated his manuscripts to a secretary. The fourth edition of *The Theory of Moral Sentiments* was published in 1774.

Despite his dedication to writing, Smith found some time for his friends. Although chided by those friends (especially Hume) for a general laxity in corresponding, he did write occasionally, particularly now that he was involved once more in requesting letters of introduction or special favors to help out his friends and family. On

June 7, 1767, Smith sent a letter to Hume seeking his assistance in helping a mutual friend. He inquired about Rousseau in the letter also. "What has become of Rousseau? Has he gone abroad, because he cannot continue to get himself sufficiently persecuted in Great Britain?" In fact, Rousseau had returned to France.

Hume sent a reply from his London home in a letter dated June 13. He ignored Smith's questions about Rousseau, however. Instead, he told of a serious quarrel between himself and Smith's childhood friend, Bishop John Oswald, which had occurred at a dinner party in James Oswald's home in England. During a conversation following dinner, Hume had jokingly complained to the group of being "very ill us'd by Lord Hertford" for the man's failure to ever appoint Hume to a position of bishop. But John did not see any humor in Hume's remark and took offense, so much so that he became enraged at Hume for insulting the distinguished Lord Hertford. In the letter to Smith, Hume spoke of being surprised and troubled that James had not intervened or apologized for his brother's rude behavior. Hume claimed that he had apologized to John, but it did no good. The furious and unforgiving John had called Hume a coward and ordered him not to return to James's home again. Hume confided to Smith that as a result of the quarrel, he believed that his lengthy friendship with James was "broke for ever."

Smith waited to respond to Hume's concerns about the disagreement with Bishop Oswald. Having been visited separately by John and James Oswald in the interim, Smith sought to explain their friend James's unwillingness, or inability, to get involved in the quarrel. Smith found out that James was seriously ill. Smith finally wrote to Hume in September from the Duke and Duchess of Buccleuch's house in Scotland:

> I cannot easily express to you the indignation with which your last letter filled me. The Bishop is a brute and a beast and unmerited preferment has rendered him, it seems, still more so. I am very much ashamed that the very great affection which I owe to his Brother [James Oswald] had ever imposed upon me so much as to give me a good opinion of him. He was at Kirkcaldy since I received your letter and I was obliged to see him, but I did not behave to him as I otherwise would have done. He thought proper to leave Edinburgh the day or the day before his brother arrived in it, without waiting to see that Brother to whom he owes everything, who was then, and is still in the most terrible distress, and who used to have no other foible so great as his esteem and regard to this haughty Blockhead. I excuse our old friend for not have taken more notice of this affair on account of the present state of his health upon which I shall explain myself to you more fully at meeting.

Hume quickly wrote back to Smith:

> I thank you for your friendly Resentment against the Right Reverend, I easily forgive our Friend [James Oswald] for not making me any Apology. Tis with great Concern I observe, that he has not Spirits enough for such an Effort, and perhaps is fetterd by some kind of Dependance on his Brute of a Brother. I have receivd two Letters from him in our usual friendly Style and have answered him in the same.

Smith stayed for a month or more with his former student at the duke's estate, Dalkieth. The duke and duchess had opened their house to guests for various social events. They were new to the area, and about fifty neighbors were invited to meet the couple and celebrate the duke's birthday on September 13. Sadly the big birthday event was postponed for a couple of weeks when the duke's stepfather, Charles Townshend, died suddenly from a fever on September 4.

Appointed to the powerful position of chancellor of the exchequer in Parliament only thirteen months before his death, Charles Townshend had managed to quickly become a controversial figure in Great Britain before he died. Lauded by some, hated by others—especially Americans—he had actively used his new position to get Parliament to increase taxes in the American colonies to help offset Great Britain's heavy debts. More importantly, Townshend had pushed to establish a board of customs

After returning to Kirkcaldy in 1767, Adam Smith lived with his mother and cousin Janet Douglas in a house on this site. That house was demolished in 1844.

in America as well. In the past, taxes collected in each American colony were sent through local agents (agents controlled by the Americans) before being passed along to revenue collectors in England. Now these tax revenues would bypass the local agents and be sent directly to an English-controlled board of customs—a board housed in America. Because the collection of taxes had been difficult to enforce in the colonies, a debate ensued in Parliament for a stronger military presence in America. Townshend argued successfully that the additional tax revenues collected from the new tax increase would help pay for the board of customs and the military enforcement needed in America.

Just a few months after Townshend had assumed the position of chancellor of the exchequer, and less than three months before the duke's birthday party, the English Parliament passed the Townshend Revenue Act. The Act had made the politically ambitious Townshend an instant celebrity in England, poised to become the next prime minister even. But Americans believed the Act unfair: it imposed even more taxes on the imports of basic goods, such as paper, glass, and tea than the detested Stamp Act (which they had eventually gotten Parliament to repeal in 1765). Nor did the Americans want a board of customs or a stronger English military presence in their country. Parliament refused to compromise, and then it made a serious strategic error. Instead of placing the board in a more accommodating and less rebellious colony such as New York, Parliament decided to put it in Boston, a hot-bed of anti-English sentiment. At the time of Townshend's sudden death, his Act had greatly increased the escalating tension between England and America.

By January 1768, Smith had left the duke's home and returned to Kirkcaldy. During that same year, James Oswald, his health continuing to decline, became too ill to work any longer, and he resigned from Parliament. The longtime close friend of Henry Home, David Hume, and Smith died soon after at the age of fifty-two.

For the next several years, Smith continued his work on *The Wealth of Nations*, in addition to revision *The Theory of Moral Sentiments*. He did plan a break to visit Hume's Edinburgh home around Christmas of 1771. Unfortunately, Hume's sister became ill with a fever and the visit did not occur.

Smith, at times, still showed his absentmindedness. One Sunday morning, Smith found himself among the local citizens dressed only in his nightdress. He had wandered for hours about town during the night deep in thought, completely unaware of what he was doing or where he was going. The citizens of Kirkcaldy were unfazed. The writer was a celebrity in his hometown, and the townspeople were accustomed to Smith's absentmindedness and strange behavior.

With the fourth edition of his *The Theory of Moral Sentiments* nearly finished, but with much left to do on *The Wealth of Nations*, Smith left Kirkcaldy and moved to London in the spring of 1773 to work closely with his publishers and complete the two manuscripts. He stopped first in Edinburgh. Still suffering periodic bouts of ill health, forty-nine-year-old Smith did not feel well, and on this occasion, he thought he had not long to live.

He began to make arrangements for his estate. In a letter dated April 16, 1773, Smith officially appointed David Hume his literary executor and provided instructions on what to do with his papers and letters should he die:

> As I have left the care of all my literary papers to you, I must tell you that except those which I carry along with me there are none worth the publishing, but a fragment of a great work which contains a history of the Astronomical Systems that were successively in fashion down to the time of Des Cartes. Whether that might not be published as a fragment of an intended juvenile work, I leave entirely to your judgement; tho I begin to suspect myself that there is more refinement than solidity in some parts of it. This little work you will find in a thin folio paper book in my writing desk in my bedroom. All the other loose papers which you will find either in that desk or within the glass folding doors of a bureau which stands in My bedroom. All the other loose papers which you will find either in that desk or within the glass folding doors of a bureau which stands in My bed room together with about eighteen thin paper folio books which you will likewise find within the same glass folding doors I desire may be destroyed without any examination. Unless I die very suddenly I shall take care that the Papers I carry with me shall be carefully sent to you. I ever am
> My Dear Friend, Most faithfully yours
> Adam Smith

But Smith's health improved and he departed Edinburgh. At the time of Smith's travels to London, each major thoroughfare leading into the city was monitored by a pikeman who collected a toll from anyone entering or leaving through one of the city's gates. Upon nearing London, the first thing one saw was a dark cloud, caused by the thick black smoke of hundreds of coal fires, persistent drizzling rain, and sometimes thick fog. The ever-present coal smoke from fireplaces in the homes and trades—where coal fires were necessary in making such products as glass, earthenware, horse-shoes and guns—blackened everything including buildings, snow, statuary, horses, and clothes.

Eighteenth-century London was not known primarily for being a manufacturing city, but rather a center for world trade. It served as the headquarters for many foreign companies, and a person could purchase such goods as Arabian gold, precious gems from Egypt, silk from China, wine from France, and Russian sable in London. There was also an active slave trade.

London was densely populated with more than 500,000 people in the mid-1700s. The streets were filled with loud and shrill sounds from a variety of activities. Cumbersome coaches lumbered noisily across the stone-paved streets, pulled by horses with steel bits jangling in their mouths, their iron-shod hooves striking the cobblestone streets. There were the cries and shouts from female and male vendors hailing customers—selling apples, oranges, pears, hot spiced gingerbreads, meat pies, books, knife-sharpening services, ale, and medicines. People on streets shouted obscenities so much that in 1746 the local government had passed a law imposing fines on anyone caught swearing. But swearing continued because London had no police force (only a national militia primarily concerned with protecting England's borders) to enforce such laws. Beggars and chimney sweeps calling out for money or work filled the streets as well.

Eighteenth-century London was a city of colorful sights. It was not unusual to see a dancing bear,

A London street scene, eighteenth century. Smith moved to London in the spring of 1773 to work closely with his publisher.

performing street actors, or a puppet show being staged in the open. Tradesmen selling gloves, hats, cheese, coal, soap, or beer hung brightly painted wooden signs outside their shops to advertise their products. Some signs were so large and heavy that a bystander risked being seriously injured if a sign fell from its hinges on a stormy, windy day.

The city had its own distinct, particular smells compared to the smaller, less densely populated towns. A bath was an infrequent luxury, and body odor a constant problem with so many pushing and shoving people crowded together in close proximity. There was also the smell of dead dogs, cats, rodents—and perhaps a horse left to decay in a dark corner—with the stench adding to the unpleasantness of the smoke-filled air, not to mention the threat of disease. While the grand market had its sweet-smelling flower, fruit, and vegetable stalls, it only took a buyer a few steps to sniff the foul odor of blood-dripping animal meats hanging from hooks. There was also the persistent stink from the Thames River and filthy city streets, which were both commonly used to dump human sewage. Homes and businesses were designed with high front steps, so that passengers could step into and out of a carriage or coach without their feet ever touching the stinking street. And although the mounds of animal dung was collected regularly and taken by barge up the congested Thames River to be used as fertilizer for the fruit and vegetable crops, the smell lingered behind.

The city, at least during the day, stayed packed with people hurrying about their business until the darkness of night and fear of crime caused the streets to empty. These massive herds of people lived mostly inside London in rented tiny rooms that were often dark and airless—with the few windows (which were considered a luxury) boarded and sealed as landlords attempted to avoid the local government's tax on windows. While water flowed to most shops and houses through pipes, few water closets or toilets could be found, except in the homes of some of the very wealthy. Bodily waste was collected in a chamber pot and carried downstairs to a basement cesspit or outside to a garden privy to be dumped. Eventually the waste was collected and removed by a worker referred to as a night soil man, although much of the sewage ended up at least temporarily in the streets and alleys.

For almost four years, Smith was one more addition to the mass of people living in London. As he had done in Paris, Smith stayed busy socializing with friends and attending the theater, lectures, and club and society meetings, including the Royal Society. In 1773, the question and talk of the town was would America and England go to war? Smith hoped war would be avoided, not only because of his concern with the destructiveness of war, but also because of the productivity and wealth for both American and England that could be realized from peaceful trade. Yet stories from America showed the flames of rebellion to be growing.

In February 1774, Smith received a letter from Hume questioning whether a mutual acquaintance of theirs, the well-known American Benjamin Franklin, could be guilty of the public charges levied against him by the English Privy Council because of an incident that had become known as the Hutchinson Affair.

Thomas Hutchinson, the English-appointed governor of Massachusetts, while publicly declaring his support of Massachusetts, was suspected by Massachusetts colonists to be secretly supporting the English Crown. In support of the colonists, Franklin, while still living in England, had gotten hold of some letters proving that Hutchinson's loyalties lay with England, and he sent them to influential friends in America. Somehow Franklin's involvement in the affair was discovered. He had appeared before the English Privy Council on January 29, 1774, and examined for the transgression of sending the inflammatory letters to Boston. At the formal examination he was condemned for being disloyal to the

On January 29, 1774, Benjamin Franklin (standing, left of center) was harangued by Attorney-General Alexander Wedderburn and heckled by members of the English Privy Council for his involvement in the Hutchinson Affair. Franklin remained silent and impassive throughout the hour-long ordeal.

Crown and publicly humiliated by Lord Wedderburn before a specially invited crowd of ladies and gentlemen that Franklin had once considered friends. Making no attempt at a defense, forced to stand before the council and the crowd for at least one hour and a half without a chance to rest, the sixty-eight-year-old distinguished statesman silently listened to the council's tirades against him.

Hume said in his letter to Smith, "How is it suppos'd, he [Franklin] got Possession of these Letters? I hear that Wedderburn's Treatment of him before the Council, was most cruel, without being in the least blameable. What a Pity!"

As England and America moved closer to war in 1774, Smith completed and published the fourth edition of *The Theory of Moral Sentiments*. He then concentrated on finishing *The Wealth of Nations*.

War between England and America seemed increasingly inevitable, although Smith maintained hope for compromise and reconciliation. But that was not to be. On September 5, 1774, the First Continental Congress convened in Philadelphia. Fifty-six delegates voted on the formation of local militia throughout the thirteen colonies. Ben Franklin had lived in London for eighteen years, and had even once considered making the city his permanent home. But England was no longer a safe place for Franklin to live, and in 1775 the diplomat sailed home to America.

George Washington surrounded by members of the Second Continental Congress, 1775. Congress unanimously chose Washington to command the Continental Army.

Smith's writing of *The Wealth of Nations* progressed slowly. He could not stop making changes to his book. Hume blamed the slowness in finalizing the book on Smith's fervent interest in the conflict between England and America. From his home in Edinburgh where he suffered from a painful, gastrointestinal illness, he wrote to Smith at his lodgings at the British Coffee-house, Charing Cross, London, on February 8, 1776:

I am as lazy a Correspondent as you; yet my anxiety about you makes me write.

By all Accounts, your Book has been printed long ago; yet it has never yet been so much as advertised. What is the Reason? If you wait till the Fate of America be decided, you may wait long.

By all accounts, you intend to settle with us this Spring: Yet we hear no more of it: What is the Reason? Your Chamber in my House is always unoccupied: I am always at home: I expect you to land here.

I have been, am, and shall be probably in an indifferent State of Health. I weighed myself t'other day, and find I have fallen five compleat Stones [one stone equals fourteen pounds]. If you delay much longer, I shall probably disappear altogether.

The Duke of Bucleugh tells me, that you are very zealous in American Affairs. My Notion is, that the Matter is not so important as is commonly imagind. If I be mistaken, I shall probably correct my Error, when I see you or read you. Our Navigation and general Commerce may suffer more than our Manufacturers. Should London fall as much in its Size, as I have done, it will be the better. It is nothing but a Hulk of bad and unclean Humours.

Finally, on March 9, 1776, *An Inquiry into the Nature and Causes of the Wealth of Nations* was published by William Strahan and Thomas Cadell of London at the cost of £1.16 per book. Adam Smith was fifty-two years old—it had taken him twelve years to write the book.

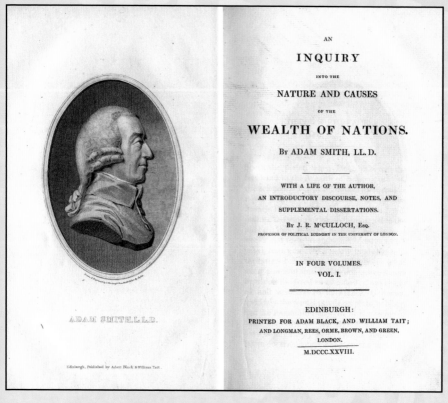

An Inquiry into the Nature and Causes of the Wealth of Nations, Smith's most famous work, was published in 1776.

Volume I had 510 pages and Volume II 587. David Hume, his health still in decline, wrote in his letter dated April 1, 1776, "Euge! Belle! Dear Mr. Smith: I am much pleas'd with your Performance, and the Perusal of it has taken me from a State of great Anxiety. It was a Work of so much Expectation, by yourself, by your Friends, and by the Public, that I trembled for its Appearance; but am now much relieved. Not but that the Reading of it necessarily requires so much Attention, and the Public is disposed to give so little, that I shall still doubt for some time of its being at first very popular."

Smith knew that Hume was very ill. Hume had been suffering on and off for many years. Fearing he would not recover this time, Hume appointed Smith his literary executor. Smith received a letter from his old friend and former colleague at Glasgow, Dr. Joseph Black, a chemist of some reputation now residing in Edinburgh. Black wrote on Hume's behalf to report his condition: "This is a Diarrhea with Colicy Pains attended with and I believe proceeding from an internal Haemorrage." Smith considered visiting Hume in June, but upon receiving word that his mother was ill, he decided to return to Kirkcaldy instead. On July 4, 1776, as America declared its independence from Great Britain and King

This 1819 painting by the American artist John Trumbull shows the Declaration of Independence being presented to the Second Continental Congress, June 28, 1776. A week later, on July 4, the Declaration was officially adopted.

George III, Hume gathered a group of close friends for a farewell dinner in Edinburgh. Smith was present.

After Hume's dinner, Smith returned to Kirkcaldy. His mother, Margaret, now in her eighties, recovered from her illness, but Hume died on August 25, 1776, at the age of sixty-five. Smith learned of his friend's death by letter from Black, who wrote that Hume had "died in such a happy composure of mind that nothing could have made it better."

Meanwhile, Hume was mistaken to worry about the popularity of *The Wealth of Nations*. Although the number of first editions printed is not known, the book sold out quickly. Smith's London publishers ordered a second printing. Smith's book was about to alter the way people thought of economics.

8 The Wealth of Nations

dam Smith was not the first to write about economics. Members of the literati had long been interested in economics and many had written on a large variety of economic issues. He was, however, among the first to write about the economy as a general system of human interaction and cooperation, one that could explain how different economic issues were all related to the overarching economic problem—motivating free people to pursue their own interests in ways that did the most to promote the interests of others. Smith's approach of developing a few general principles and then using those principles to provide insights into a large variety of economic concerns made *The Wealth of Nations* much more important than any economics book that had been written previously.

Smith's book exposed the weaknesses of the mercantilist system. To Smith, the wealth of a nation was best measured by the well-being of ordinary people, not by the wealth of kings and queens, large landowners, or even business people. According to Smith,

> Servants, labourers, and workmen of different kinds, make up the far greater part of every great political society. But

what improves the circumstances of the greater part can never be regarded as an inconveniency to the whole. No society can surely be flourishing and happy, of which the far greater part of the members are poor and miserable. It is but equity, besides, that they who feed, cloath and lodge the whole body of the people, should have such a share of the produce of their own labour as to be themselves tolerably well fed, cloathed and lodged.

Opposed to what the mercantilists believed, Smith emphasized that a nation's wealth was ultimately the result not of having a lot of gold, or other precious metals, or of the profits of businesses, but of how much people had to consume. He wrote:

> Consumption is the sole end and purpose of all production; and the interest of the producer ought to be attended to, only so far as it may be necessary for promoting that of the consumer. The maxim is so perfectly self-evident, that it would be absurd to attempt to prove it. But in the mercantile system, the interest of the consumer is almost constantly sacrificed to that of the producer.

A prime example to Smith of sacrificing the interest of the consumer to that of producers was tariff duties on foreign goods, which increased the cost to consumers to protect the high prices charged by domestic producers against foreign competition. Mercantilists argued that tariff duties allowed domestic producers to sell more to foreign countries than domestic consumers bought from foreign countries. This resulted in more money (typically in the form of gold and silver) flowing into the country than flowed out, with the buildup of precious metals increasing the nation's wealth. But Smith disagreed, and he argued "that wealth does not consist in money, or in gold and silver; but in what money purchases, and is valuable only for purchasing."

The importance of consumption means that production is also important since things have to be produced before they can be purchased and consumed. No matter how much money a country has, it is worth nothing without something to spend it on. A country that produces nothing will not even be able to buy products from productive countries, at least not for long. Productive countries are willing to produce things for another country not

In *The Wealth of Nations*, Smith posited that a country's wealth was not measured by how much gold or other precious metals were stockpiled in its treasury, or by the size of its business profits, but by the quantity of goods available for its people to consume.

because they want the country's money, but because they want to buy the products it produces. Unless a country produces goods and services, it has nothing to sell, and therefore its money has little value to consumers in other countries.

Because Smith understood the importance of consumption, he also recognized that the wealth of a nation depends on how productive its workers are. Smith

An eighteenth-century watercolor of a forge, with each worker performing a different task. Smith considered the division of labor one of the most important factors in high productivity.

wrote, "The greatest improvement in the productive powers of labour, and the greater part of the skill, dexterity, and judgment with which it is any where directed, or applied, seem to have been the effects of the division of labour." He illustrates the productivity resulting from the division of labor with the example of a pin factory—which he had observed as a boy in Kirkcaldy. Smith explained how several different workers specialized (divided their labor) in several different steps to make a pin—"One man draws out the wire, another straights it, a third cuts it, a fourth points it, a fifth grinds it at the top for receiving the head; to make the head requires two or three distinct operations . . . and the important business of making a pin is, in this manner, divided into about eighteen distinct operations." In this way, Smith says that he has seen ten men "make among them upwards of forty-eight thousand pins in a day." In contrast, Smith states that "if they had all wrought separately and independently, and without any of them having been educated to this particular business, they certainly could not each of them have made twenty, perhaps not one pin in a day."

Smith identified three reasons for the "great increase of the quantity of work" resulting from the division of labor: "first, to the increase of dexterity in every particular workman; secondly, to the saving of the time which is commonly lost in passing from one species of work to another; and lastly, to the invention of a great number of machines which facilitate and abridge labour, and enable one man to do the work of many."

But despite the enormous increase in output from the division of labor, there is a serious coordination problem resulting from workers specializing in narrow productive activities, and Smith devoted much of *The Wealth of Nations* to addressing this problem. He recognized that the division of labor makes sense only if the market—say for pins—contains a large number of people. As Smith pointed out, "When the market is very small, no person can have any encouragement to dedicate himself entirely to one employment, for want of the power to exchange all that surplus part of the produce of his own labour, which is over and above his own consumption, for such parts of the produce of other men's labour as he has occasion for."

The coordination problem is, how do specialized workers, producing far more of a product than they want to consume, know how much of their production others want to consume? There is little benefit in specializing in the production of thousands and thousands of pins, for example, unless other people want those pins and will buy them. And how do people, who because they have specialized in producing just one, or part of one product, communicate their consumption desires to the millions of other specialized workers whom they depend on for almost everything they consume? Even if a worker knows what others want, there is little benefit in specializing to produce it without some assurance that others are producing the things that he or she wants.

Getting millions of people throughout the world to somehow coordinate their production and consumption decisions is a serious problem. Every day workers go to their job and specialize in the production of products without anyone ever telling them who wants that product, or how much they want. Those workers then use the money they are paid to buy the products that they want without needing to tell anyone about their consumption plans. From his years of observing people's behavior, Smith knew that men and women in the cities did not provide advance notification to farmers regarding what crops, and how much of each crop, to produce every year. He knew that the Scotsman did not mail a letter to the ship captain in advance telling him how many crates of wine to smuggle to the Scottish shore. How then, Smith wondered, does all this social cooperation happen?

Smith believed the answer is found in the coordination motivated by market prices and profits. When consumers want more of a good than producers are willing to supply at the prevailing price, competition among consumers will cause the price, and producer profits, to increase. As the price increases, consumers will reduce the amount they wish to buy and producers will increase the amount they wish to sell. Eventually the price reaches the level where the amount being produced is equal to the amount people want, and there is no more upward pressure on the price.

And the opposite price adjustment occurs when consumers want less of a product than producers want to sell at the existing price. In this case, competition among producers causes the price of the product to fall. As the price falls, consumers desire to buy more of the

A farming plantation, late 1700s. How, Smith asked in *The Wealth of Nations*, do producers such as farmers know what to produce and in what quantities? His answer: market prices and profits.

good and producers are willing to supply less. Eventually the price declines to the level where the amount consumers want to buy and producers want to sell are equal, and the price ceases to decline.

Smith summarized this process: "When the quantity brought to market is just sufficient to supply the effectual demand and no more, the market price naturally comes to be either exactly, or as nearly as can be judged of, the same with the natural price." Smith defined "natural price" as the price of a product that "is neither more nor less than what is sufficient to pay the rent of the land, the wages of the labour, and the profits of the stock employed in raising, preparing, and bringing it to market . . ." In other words, the natural price just covers the cost of making the product available to consumers. This process of coordination includes the investments people make and the jobs they take. Regarding jobs, Smith wrote, "If in the same neighbourhood, there was any employment evidently either more or less advantageous than the rest, so many people would crowd into it in the one case, and so many would desert it in the other, that its advantages would soon return to the level of the other employments."

It is this coordination and cooperation that Adam Smith described in his famous passage on the "invisible hand." In pursuing his own objectives, each individual "intends only his own gain, and he is in this, as in many other cases, led by an invisible hand to promote an end which was no part of his intention. Nor is it always the worse for society that it was no part of it. By pursuing his own interest he frequently promotes that of the society more effectually than when he really intends to promote it."

The social and economic coordination that Smith describes takes place simultaneously with respect to many thousands of products, investments and jobs when people are free to pursue their own objectives while respecting the property rights of others and abiding by the rules of voluntary exchange. This coordination could never be achieved through the direction of government authorities. No government could ever keep track of all the changes in technologies, preferences, and conditions that affect the decisions that are best for each person, or know how those decisions can best be coordinated over the many millions of people affected. This is a point that Smith particularly emphasized:

> The statesman, who should attempt to direct private people in what manner they ought to employ their capitals, would not only load himself with a most unnecessary attention, but assume an authority which could safely be trusted, not only to no single person, but to no council or senate whatever, and which would nowhere be so dangerous as in the hands of a man who had folly and presumption enough to fancy himself fit to exercise it.

Because of the coordination of the market, people benefit from the productivity made possible by the specialized efforts of hundreds of millions of other people from all over the world. Even the simplest items would be either unavailable or extremely expensive without the coordinated effort of enormous numbers of widely dispersed people. According to Smith, "Observe the accommodation of the most common artificer or day-labourer in a civilized and thriving country, and you will perceive that the number of people of whose industry a part, though but a small part, has been employed in procuring him this accommodation, exceeds all computation . . ." Smith continues this sentence with almost two pages in which he lists some of the specialized workers in a large number of different occupations whose joint efforts are required to provide a "coarse and rough" woolen coat for a "day-labourer."

Smith did not believe that people were greedy materialists who think only about themselves, as he explained in *The Theory of Moral Sentiments*. But in *The Wealth of Nations* he was interested in how millions of people spread all over the world managed to cooperate for their mutual benefit, and he recognized that such cooperation could not result from all those people knowing and caring about each other. So in *The Wealth of Nations* Smith emphasizes the importance of appealing not to the benevolence of the multitude of people whom people depend upon for most of the things they consume, but to their self-interest. This emphasis is summarized in what has become one of Smith's most quoted passages: "It is not from the benevolence of the butcher, the brewer, or the baker, that we expect our dinner, but from their regard to their own interest. We address ourselves, not to their humanity but to their self-love, and never talk to them of our own necessities but of their advantages."

The trade that Smith saw as the basis for the division of labor and the widespread cooperation that greatly increases the wealth of a nation is not limited to domestic trade. Just as trade within a country makes it possible for people to produce what they are best at producing and get from others what they are best at producing, so foreign trade allows this specialization to be extended over many countries. Attempting to produce in one country what can be produced at less cost in another reduces the total value of what can be produced and consumed, and therefore reduces the wealth of the nation. As Smith points out:

> By means of glasses, hotbeds, and hotwalls, very good grapes can be raised in Scotland, and very good wine too can be made of them at about thirty times the expence for which at least equally good can be brought from foreign countries. Would it be a reasonable law to prohibit the importation of all foreign wines, merely to encourage the making of claret and burgundy in Scotland?

For Smith, the answer was no. For example, Scotland could get far more wine for a given amount of effort and resources by producing wool (which it produced at far less cost than wine) in excess of what the people of Scotland needed for themselves, and trading the extra wool for wine from France and Spain (which they produced at far less cost than wool). The fear that trade with foreign countries destroys domestic employment was not seen by Smith as an overriding concern. Of course, some Scottish jobs would be destroyed in wine production if Scotland imported wine from France, but more productive jobs would be created in wool production when the money the French received from selling wine to the Scottish was used to import wool produced in Scotland. As Smith explained:

The interest of a nation in its commercial relations to foreign nations is, like that of a merchant with regard to the different people with whom he deals, to buy as cheap and to sell as dear as possible. But it will be most likely to buy cheap, when by the most perfect freedom of trade it encourages all nations to bring to it the goods which it has occasion to purchase; and, for the same reason, it will be most likely to sell dear, when its markets are thus filled with the greatest number of buyers.

It is true that moving from restrictions on foreign trade to free trade requires that some workers make difficult relocations to new jobs. Smith was fully aware of this problem and recommended that a move to free trade be made gradually in situations where a large amount of unemployment, even though temporary, would otherwise occur. As much as Smith wanted free

Although his countrymen consumed their share of wine, Smith argued that it did not make sense to produce wine in Scotland because doing so would cost much more than importing wine from France or Spain. Scotland could obtain far more wine for a given amount of resources by trading a product it produced cheaply, such as wool, with a wine-producing country.

trade, he also felt that "Humanity may in this case require that the freedom of trade should be restored only by slow gradations, and with a good deal of reserve and circumspection."

Smith perceived the biggest obstacle to free trade to be the influence of large businesses, whose owners (the merchants and manufacturers) wanted to protect their jobs and products against competition from foreign producers. As an advocate for the ordinary consumer, Smith pointed out that "In every country it always is and must be the interest of the great body of the people to buy whatever they want of those who sell it cheapest." Smith then explained that the interests of businesses are "directly opposite to that of the great body of the people. As it is the interest of the freemen of a corporation to hinder the rest of the inhabitants from employing any workmen but themselves, so it is the interest of the merchants and manufacturers of every country to secure to themselves the monopoly of the home market." Smith recognized that consumers are at a disadvantage in this conflict with business. Consumers buy large numbers of different products and therefore have little motivation to organize and lobby politicians to maintain competition in the supply of any particular one of those products. On the other hand, each business merchant selling a particular product has a strong motivation to lobby politicians to protect himself against competition.

Smith's views regarding free trade extended to the British colonies, including America. The mercantilist economic policy of Britain in 1776 was largely influenced by merchants and manufacturers who got laws passed requiring the colonists to sell their raw materials to England and to buy their finished goods from England. Smith argued that these restrictions on free trade with the American and West Indian colonies benefited English business far less than it cost English consumers in higher prices and taxes—"in the system of laws which has been established for the management of our American and West Indian colonies, the interest of the home-consumer has been sacrificed to that of the producer with a more extravagant profusion than in all our other commercial regulations."

Although he was sympathetic to the American situation, he did not want a war between America and England. Instead, he favored a union between the two countries, and in other colonies in which ideally Great Britain would "give up all authority over her colonies, and leave them to elect their own magistrates, to enact their own laws, and to make peace and war as they might think proper." According to Smith, if such a relationship were adopted, "Great Britain would not only be immediately freed from the whole annual expence of the peace establishment of the colonies, but might settle with them such treaty of commerce as would effectually secure to her a free trade, more advantageous to the great body of the people, though less so to the merchants, than the monopoly which she at present enjoys."

The Wealth of Nations has remained famous and relevant for well over two hundred years because in it Smith developed an organized framework for understanding economics that is still applicable today. The division of

Page 256 — Wheat per quarter.

Years		£	s.	d.	Years		£	s.	d.
1637,	—	2	13	0	Brought over,	—	79	14	10
1638,	—	2	17	0	1671,	—	2	2	0
1639,	—	2	4	10	1672,	—	2	1	0
1640,	—	2	4	8	1673,	—	2	6	8
1641,	—	2	8	0	1674,	—	3	8	8
1642,	—	0	0	0	1675,	—	3	4	8
1643,	—	0	0	0	1676,	—	1	18	0
1644,	—	0	0	0	1677,	—	2	2	0
1645,	—	0	0	0	1678,	—	2	19	0
1646,	—	2	8	0	1679,	—	3	0	0
1647,	—	3	13	8	1680,	—	2	5	0
1648,	—	4	5	0	1681,	—	2	6	8
1649,	—	4	0	0	1682,	—	2	4	0
1650,	—	3	16	8	1683,	—	2	0	0
1651,	—	3	13	4	1684,	—	2	4	0
1652,	—	2	9	6	1685,	—	2	6	8
1653,	—	1	15	6	1686,	—	1	14	0
1654,	—	1	6	0	1687,	—	1	5	2
1655,	—	1	13	4	1688,	—	2	6	0
1656,	—	2	3	0	1689,	—	1	10	0
1657,	—	2	6	8	1690,	—	1	14	8
1658,	—	3	5	0	1691,	—	1	14	0
1659,	—	3	6	0	1692,	—	2	6	8
1660,	—	2	16	6	1693,	—	3	7	8
1661,	—	3	10	0	1694,	—	3	4	0
1662,	—	3	14	0	1695,	—	2	13	0
1663,	—	2	17	0	1696,	—	3	11	0
1664,	—	2	0	6	1697,	—	3	0	0
1665,	—	2	9	4	1698,	—	3	8	4
1666,	—	1	16	0	1699,	—	3	4	0
1667,	—	1	16	0	1700,	—	2	0	0
1668,	—	2	0	0					
1669,	—	2	4	4			60)	153	1	8
1670,	—	2	1	8				2	11	0½
Carry over,		79	14	10						

[Left margin note at 1642–1645: Wanting in the account. The supplied by Bishop Fleetwood.]

Page 257 — Wheat per quarter.

Years		£	s.	d.	Years		£	s.	d.
1701,	—	1	17	8	Brought over,	—	69	8	8
1702,	—	1	9	6	1734,	—	1	18	10
1703,	—	1	16	0	1735,	—	2	3	0
1704,	—	2	6	6	1736,	—	2	0	4
1705,	—	1	10	0	1737,	—	1	18	0
1706,	—	1	6	0	1738,	—	1	15	6
1707,	—	1	8	6	1739,	—	1	18	6
1708,	—	2	1	6	1740,	—	2	10	8
1709,	—	3	18	6	1741,	—	2	6	8
1710,	—	3	18	0	1742,	—	1	14	0
1711,	—	2	14	0	1743,	—	1	4	10
1712,	—	2	6	4	1744,	—	1	4	10
1713,	—	2	11	0	1745,	—	1	7	6
1714,	—	2	10	4	1746,	—	1	19	0
1715,	—	2	3	0	1747,	—	1	14	10
1716,	—	2	8	0	1748,	—	1	17	0
1717,	—	2	5	8	1749,	—	1	17	0
1718,	—	1	18	10	1750,	—	1	12	6
1719,	—	1	15	0	1751,	—	1	18	6
1720,	—	1	17	0	1752,	—	2	1	10
1721,	—	1	17	6	1753,	—	2	4	8
1722,	—	1	16	0	1754,	—	1	14	8
1723,	—	1	14	8	1755,	—	1	13	10
1724,	—	1	17	0	1756,	—	2	5	3
1725,	—	2	8	6	1757,	—	3	0	0
1726,	—	2	6	0	1758,	—	2	10	0
1727,	—	2	2	0	1759,	—	1	19	10
1728,	—	2	14	6	1760,	—	1	16	6
1729,	—	2	6	10	1761,	—	1	10	3
1730,	—	1	16	6	1762,	—	1	19	0
1731,	—	1	12	10	1763,	—	2	0	9
1732,	—	1	6	8	1764,	—	2	6	9
1733,	—	1	8	4					
Carry over,		69	8	8			64)	129	13	6
								2	0	6[13/32]¹

Wheat per quarter.

Years		£	s.	d.	Years		£	s.	d.
1731,	—	1	12	10	1741,	—	2	6	8
1732,	—	1	6	8	1742,	—	1	14	0
1733,	—	1	8	4	1743,	—	1	4	10
1734,	—	1	18	10	1744,	—	1	4	10
1735,	—	2	3	0	1745,	—	1	7	6
1736,	—	2	0	4	1746,	—	1	19	0
1737,	—	1	18	0	1747,	—	1	14	10
1738,	—	1	15	6	1748,	—	1	17	0
1739,	—	1	18	6	1749,	—	1	17	0
1740,	—	2	10	8	1750,	—	1	12	6
		10)	18	12	8		10)	16	18	2
			1	17	3½			1	13	9¾

¹[This should be 13/32.]

VOL. I.—17

This table, one of many in *The Wealth of Nations*, records wheat prices by year. Smith's book has remained relevant because of the author's organized framework for understanding economics.

labor, market cooperation and coordination, the importance of the ordinary consumer, and advantages of free trade are fundamental insights that Adam Smith provided into the nature and causes of economic prosperity. These insights are crucial to an informed appreciation of the overarching concern of economics—that is, how free people from all over the world can, given certain broad social and political rules, cooperate with each other in ways that promote the prosperity of all.

9

An Advocate for free Trade

Smith lived in Kirkcaldy until January of 1777, when he returned to London for most of that year to revise *The Wealth of Nations*. Mainly educated men and women, especially the literati, read the first edition. Unlike the writings of well-known literati such as Shaftesbury, Sidney, Locke, Hutcheson, and even Hume, Smith's book was not considered controversial, in part because he had written nothing to offend any religious officials. Nor did it excite controversy or much interest on the part of many politicians, who dismissed the suggestions in *The Wealth of Nations* as the impractical ideas of a bookworm professor.

There was one notable exception, however. Lord North, serving in the combined roles of prime minister and chancellor of the exchequer of Great Britain, found in the treatise a wealth of ideas for raising taxes to finance the expensive war with the American colonies. He took Smith's recommendations in *The Wealth of Nations* seriously enough to get Parliament to impose two new taxes in 1777—one on man-servants and a second on property sold by auction. The following year Lord North got Parliament to impose two more taxes recommended in Smith's book—on malt and inhabited houses. How Smith felt about having his ideas on taxation used to finance a war he opposed is not known.

In recognition of his outstanding contribution to Great Britain—a recognition supported, if not first requested, by the Duke of Buccleuch—Smith was awarded the positions of commissioner of customs and commissioner of the salt duties in Edinburgh. The two appointments paid Smith an annual salary of £600. Following in the footsteps of his father and other relatives

Lord North, the British prime minister, used Smith's ideas in *The Wealth of Nations* to introduce a series of new taxes to fund Britain's war against America.

(including Hercules Scott Smith in Kirkcaldy and another Adam Smith, customs official in Alloa, Scotland), Smith enthusiastically agreed to accept responsibility for enforcing trade laws and collecting taxes in Scotland. A rather odd decision, said some, for a person who had just published a book advocating free trade and eliminating mercantilism.

Smith officially started his new job in early 1778. He sought to give up his pension from the Duke of Buccleuch, but the duke refused. Smith's income from the increasing sales of his books was beginning to show a significant return. At the age of fifty-four the former professor, one-time traveling tutor, and distinguished author had become a prosperous and affluent government bureaucrat. And he had become a man who associated comfortably not only within a circle of intellectual friends, but with politicians, such as Prime Minister Lord North and Attorney General Alexander Wedderburn.

About the time the second edition of *The Wealth of Nations* was published in early 1778, Smith moved his belongings from Kirkcaldy to Edinburgh, accompanied by his mother Margaret and cousin Janet. He took a house named after the Panmure family who had lived there before him. Many friends lived in Edinburgh, including some who resided in the same area of the city as Panmure House. Smith's longtime friend eighty-two-year-old Henry Home, who had sponsored Smith's Edinburgh lectures on rhetoric and belles lettres back in 1748, lived in Edinburgh as well, although in another part of the city. Once Smith and the women had settled in their new home, David Douglas of Strathendry, Margaret's nephew, moved into Panmure House to live with them and attend college.

As he had been in carrying out his administrative duties at the University of Glasgow, Smith was conscientious and diligent in his new bureaucratic duties as a commissioner. The five commissioners met approximately four times a week, and in the first year of his appointment Smith attended 169 meetings. The commissioners were authorized by Parliament to see that mercantilism and trade policies were enforced. Smuggling and other violations of customs laws occurred regularly (such as a ship captain evading taxes by not declaring all of his goods), and the commissioners had the power to set penalties on violators. Extensive minutes were maintained of commission meeting activities that ranged from the day-to-day minutiae of collecting taxes in the city of Edinburgh to advising and preparing trade bills for Parliament.

The idea of the moral philosopher and author of *The Wealth of Nations* becoming a tax collector—enforcing many of the mercantilist policies he opposed—seemed ironic to certain members of the literati. Some were perplexed, some embarrassed. Edward Gibbon, an influential historian and author of *The Decline and Fall of the Roman Empire*, sent Smith a note of congratulation in which he wrote:

> Among the strange reports, which are every day circulated in this wide town, I heard one to-day so very extraordinary, that I know not how to give credit to it. I was informed that a place of Commissioner of the Customs in Scotland had been given to a Philosopher who for his own glory and for the benefit of mankind had enlightened the world by the most profound and systematic treatise on the great objects of trade and revenue which had ever been published in any age or in any Country. But as I was told at the same time that this Philosopher was my particular friend, I found myself very forcible inclined to believe, what I most sincerely wished and desired.

Smith may have enthusiastically accepted his new role as trade enforcer, but that had not changed his views on the importance of free trade among countries. As the author of *The Wealth of Nations* and now a government bureaucrat with firsthand knowledge of Great

A view of Edinburgh in the late 1700s. Smith moved to Edinburgh in 1778 after gaining the positions of commissioner of customs and commissioner of the salt duties there.

Britain's mercantilist policies, he was regularly consulted by government officials.

Two countries that immediately benefited from his views were France and Ireland. France and Great Britain had been enemies for centuries. The Stuarts, once dethroned from England, had taken refuge in France. The Scots, Irish, Americans, and other countries within the British Empire were forbidden from trading directly with France. But the relationship between France and England began to warm in 1778–1779 when William Eden, commissioner for conciliation with America and a political ally of Prime Minister Lord North and Attorney General Alexander Wedderburn, negotiated a commercial treaty with France based on Book IV, Chapter iii of *The Wealth of Nations*. In this chapter Smith had written, "It is in consequence of these maxims [mercantilist policies] that the commerce between France and England has in both countries been subjected to so many discouragements and restraints. If those two countries, however, were to consider their real interest, without either mercantile jealousy or national animosity, the commerce of France might be more advantageous to Great Britain than that of any other country, and for the same reason that of Great Britain to France."

Regarding Ireland, Lord Carlisle (First Lord of Trade and Plantations), the politician Lord Henry Dundas, and others requested Smith's opinion on a more serious matter confronting Great Britain: granting the Irish their wish for free trade, including imports as well as exports. Smith wrote to Lord Carlisle, "I cannot believe a [sic] that the interest of Britain would be hurt by it [granting Ireland free trade]. On the contrary, the Competition of Irish goods in the British market might contribute to break down in Part that monopoly which we have most absurdly granted to the greater part of our own workmen against ourselves."

Yet Parliament hesitated in granting the Irish free trade because they feared other countries within the British Empire would want free trade also. On the other hand, there was an expensive war being waged across the ocean in America. Irish recruits had joined the revolutionary army in America and the Irish had raised an illegal army. The last thing England wanted while waging an expensive war in America was the added cost of a war with Ireland. Writing to Lord Dundas, Smith said, "I should think it madness not to grant it." In 1779, the Irish were granted free trade rights.

Smith was carried by sedan chair or walked to his office at the Custom House in the morning. Of average height, he had a round belly, a large nose and big teeth. Dressed in the style of the time, he usually wore a light-colored coat, knee-breeches, white silk stockings, and buckle shoes and wore a flat broad-brimmed beaver hat on his powdered wig. He carried a walking staff. His old habits had not changed, and he frequently talked to himself while walking down the street, unless pausing to smile and converse with an acquaintance or to address a street vendor.

Both official and personal duties kept him busy. In a letter to Andreas Holt, commissioner of the Danish board of trade economy, Smith wrote, "I am ashamed of having delayed so long to answer your very obliging letter; but I am occupied four days in every Week at the Custom House; during which it is impossible to sit down seriously to any other business: during the other three days too, I am liable to be frequently interrupted by the extraordinary duties of my office, as well as by my own private affairs, and the common duties of society."

Smith had everything he could ever want in Edinburgh: a job he relished (despite the time it required), club and society meetings to attend, and financial security. He had authority and influence among prominent members of the nobility and government that he could use to help promote his ideas on liberty and free trade. He had a loving family, a home frequently filled with friends and visiting dignitaries who would meet for Sunday suppers, and a library of books—at least 3,000. His personal library included books on travel, literature, art, Latin and Greek classics, law, politics, biographies, political economy, history, science, philosophy, even poetry. Books on theology included the Bible and a French translation of the Koran.

During these years spent in Edinburgh, Smith often met with his two closest friends: his former colleague at Glasgow, Dr. Joseph Black and noted geologist Dr. James Hutton. These three would join other friends at two o'clock on Friday afternoon at a local tavern known for its oysters to eat dinner and engage in intellectual conversation. Eventually this Friday meeting became officially recognized as the Oyster Club.

Panmure House in Edinburgh, where Smith lived from 1778 to 1790.

An engraving of a 1790 print of Adam Smith.

By 1781, *The Wealth of Nations* had been translated into several languages—Danish, French, Italian, and German. In addition to his commissioner duties, Smith began revising his book for a third edition. He wrote to his publisher, Thomas Cadell:

> I have many apologies to make to you for my Idleness since I came to Scotland. The truth is, I bought at London a good many, partly new books, and partly either new editions of old books, or editions that were new to me; and the amusement I found in reading and diverting myself with them debauched me from proper business; the preparing a new edition of the Wealth of nations [sic]. I am now, however, heartily engaged at my proper work and I hope in two or three months to send you up the second Edition corrected in many places, with three or four very considerable additions; chiefly to the second volume; among the rest is a short, but I flatter myself, a compleat History of all the trading companies in G. Britain.

Upon reaching the age of fifty-nine and feeling well enough to remain active, Smith continued to help his friends and family—whether such help involved writing a letter to Edmund Burke, supporting the man's stand on a particular political issue, or writing Edward Gibbon recommending an acquaintance for a position as a professor of Greek at the University of Edinburgh. Smith continued to support various clubs and societies, and in 1783 he helped found the Royal Society of Edinburgh, an organization for the cultivation of science. Unfortunately, Smith had reached the age where he was losing many of his longtime close friends. Henry Home died on December 27, 1782, at the age of eighty-six.

During illness or good health, Smith was an enthusiastic participator in whatever job he undertook, whether it involved additional administrative duties at the University of Glasgow or the Scottish Customs Commission. He tried to be honest and fair in his dealings with others, especially when they involved finances—from trying to return his students' tuition when he departed the University of Glasgow, to being willing to forego the pension he had been promised the Duke of Buccleuch upon his appointment to a commissioner of customs. And he was conscientious and meticulous with his own finances. He often wrote letters to his London publishers, Thomas Cadell and William Strahan, on matters of money pertaining to the sales of his books among other business matters. He once wrote to Strahan, "You have made a small mistake in stating our account; you credit me with £150 only, instead of £170; the first bill being £120 the second for £50. Cadell, however, still remains unpaid. As soon as I understand he has delivered the books, or before it, if he will send me the account of them, I shall send him the money." And in another letter to Strahan:

I think it is predestined that I shall never write a letter to you; except to ask some favour of you, or to put you to some trouble. This letter is not to depart from the style of all the rest. I am a subscriber for Watts copying machine. The price is six Guineas for the machine and five Shillings for the packing box; I should be glad too [if] he would send me a ream of the copying Paper, together with all the other specimens of Ink etc. which commonly accompany the Machine. For payment of this to Mr. Woodmason, the seller, whose printed letter I have enclosed, you will herewith receive a bill of eight Guineas payable at sight. [The Watt referenced is Smith's friend, the man credited with improving the steam engine.]

When the third edition of *The Wealth of Nations* was about to be completed, Smith wrote to Strahan about taking a leave of absence from his duties as commissioner to live in London for four months. But Smith decided he could not make the trip because he needed to loan money to a relative instead. He wrote to Strahan, "I intended to have asked a four months leave of absence . . . in order to have attended the reprinting of my Book. But a Welch Nephew of mine tells me that unless I advance him two hundred pounds he must sell his commission in the army. This robs me of the money with which I intended to defray the expence of my expedition."

By 1783, the war between America and Great Britain had ended. America had successfully won independence. Now the Americans had to figure out what to do with thirteen separate colonies, with it not clear that they could come together as one nation. As the Americans began their struggle to form a nation that would benefit enormously from embracing many of the policies advocated in *The Wealth of Nations*, life was good for Smith. He had a job as a commissioner of customs that he enjoyed, enough time and good health to work on revisions of his two books, and the respect of many friends and associates. Smith was also blessed with a happy home life with his cousin, a loving mother, and her nephew.

10 The Author of *The Wealth of Nations* Lies Here

argaret Douglas Smith died on May 23, 1784. She was ninety. Mother and son had been devoted to one another for sixty years. Smith did not recover easily from his mother's death, in part because of his own failing health, and he fell into a depression. When Smith wrote to William Strahan in June 1784 regarding proofs for the third edition of *The Wealth of Nations*, he mentioned the death of his mother. "I must say to you, what I have said to other people, that the final separation from a person who certainly loved me more than any other person ever did or ever will love me; and whom I certainly loved and respected more than I ever shall either love or respect any other person, I cannot help feeling, even at this hour, as a very heavy stroke upon me." Fortunately he still had his cousin Janet and nephew David Douglas to offer companionship, and he continued to attend commission meetings.

This statue of Adam Smith was erected on Edinburgh's Royal Mile in 2008.

ADAM
SMITH

The third edition of *The Wealth of Nations* was published in 1784, and Smith began working on a fourth edition. It would be Strahan's last collaboration with Smith: Strahan died on July 9, 1785. Smith had suffered many losses—Hutcheson, Hume, Kames, Oswald, Strahan, and his mother Margaret. "My friends grow very thin in the world, and I do not find that my new ones are likely to supply their place," he said.

The fourth edition of *The Wealth of Nations* was published in 1786. That same year Smith became seriously ill with an intestinal ailment that lingered for some time. He attended only seventy-seven Customs Commission meetings in 1787, and the usually stout Smith lost a significant amount of weight.

In 1787, Smith met with Prime Minister William Pitt. They discussed reforming Britain's tax system in keeping with Smith's ideas in *The Wealth of Nations*.

Once he had recovered sufficiently to travel, Smith visited London in April. There he met William Pitt, who had become prime minister of Great Britain in 1783. Pitt was seeking to reform the nation's process of taxing and spending in ways consistent with the recommendations in *The Wealth of Nations*. The two men met often during Smith's visit to London. In one particular meeting with Pitt and other dignitaries, Smith arrived after the others. As he entered the room the entire group stood to show their respect. Smith asked the gentlemen to be seated. But the men waited, with Pitt saying that as we are all your scholars, they would remain standing until Dr. Smith was seated.

Soon after his return to Edinburgh, Smith was chosen lord rector at the University of Glasgow, a recognition based on merit. This appointment meant a lot to Smith, because it required the support of both university professors and students. Upon being notified of the appointment, Smith wrote to the Reverend Dr. Archibald Davidson, principal of the college:

I accept with gratitude and pleasure the very great honour which the University of Glasgow have done me in electing me for the ensuing year to be the Rector of that illustrious Body. No preferment could have given me so much real satisfaction. No man can own greater obligations to a Society than I do to the University of Glasgow. They educated me, they sent me to Oxford, soon after my return to Scotland they elected me one of their own members, and afterwards preferred me to another office, to which the abilities and Virtues of the never to be forgotten Dr. Hutcheson had given a superior degree of illustration. The period of thirteen years which I spent as a member of that society, I remember as by far the most useful and, therefore, as by far the happiest and most honourable period of my life; and now, after three and twenty years absence, to be remembered in so very agreeable a manner by my old friends and Protectors give me a heartfelt joy which I cannot easily express to you.

I shall be happy to receive the commands of my Colleagues concerning the time when it may be convenient for them to do me the honour of admitting me to the office. Mr. Millar mentions Christmas. We have commonly at the Board of Customs a vacation of five or six days at that time. But I am so regular an attendant that I think myself entitled to take the play for a week at any time. It will be no inconveniency to me, therefore, to wait upon you at whatever time you please. I beg to be remembered to my Colleagues in the most respectful and the most affectionate manner; and that you would believe me to be, with great truth, Reverend and Dear Sir,

Your and their most obliged
most obedient and most humble Servant
Adam Smith.

The installation ceremony as rector of the University of Glasgow was held on December 12, 1787. Smith was re-elected for a second term, and held this honorable position for two years.

By spring of 1788, Smith's health had greatly improved, although he missed many commission meetings that year, primarily because he took a four-month leave of absence to write. Sadly, he suffered another tragic loss when his cousin, Janet Douglas, died in the fall. David Douglas was at the University of Glasgow and could now visit only during the holidays. Smith had no close family members to keep him company any longer. In the winter his health began to worsen again, and he managed to attend about half of the commission meetings in 1789, although he did manage to work on a major revision of *The Theory of Moral Sentiments*.

In 1789, Smith published the fifth edition of *The Wealth of Nations* and continued to finalize the expanded sixth edition of *The Theory of Moral Sentiments*. The book was published in May 1790. Smith wrote to Thomas Cadell on May 25 that "I expected by this time to have been setting out upon my Journey to London. But my progress to recovery is so very slow, and so often interrupted by violent relapses that the probability of my being able to execute that Journey becomes every day more doubtful."

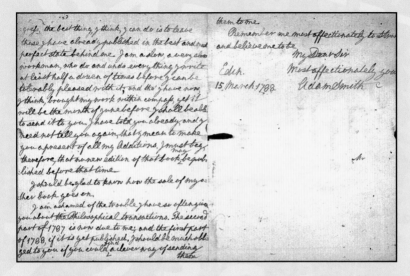

In this March 15, 1788, letter to his publisher Thomas Cadell, Adam Smith admitted, "I am a slow, a very slow workman, who do and undo everything I write at least half a dozen of times before I can be tolerably pleased with it."

Smith appointed close friends Joseph Black and James Hutton his literary executors and asked them to destroy his letters and papers—before his death. They delayed, believing he might recover from illness and change his mind. Smith repeated his request and finally the two executors reluctantly met with him at Panmure House. Without knowing what his papers contained they burned them all. The only exception was Smith's papers on astronomy, which after years of work had yet to be completed and published.

Smith complained of being in pain and his friends worried about his failing health. Still, he fulfilled his obligations as best he could. He had not yet resigned his commissioner position, and continued to attend some meetings. He also maintained contact with friends.

Smith's grave in the churchyard at Canongate, Edinburgh. This stone was erected in 2008 to replace Smith's original headstone.

On the evening of July 13, 1790, the seriously ailing Smith was at home having supper with friends when he excused himself early to go to bed. Four days later, on July 17, he died at home at the age of sixty-seven.

He was buried in Canongate churchyard, Edinburgh. The words on his original headstone were simple: Adam Smith, author of *The Wealth of Nations*, lies here.

David Douglas was the sole heir to Smith's estate. David did not inherit the rich estate his uncle was thought to have accumulated, however. Smith had given much of his wealth to charities that supported the poor.

Adam Smith's works are still read today, and his theories on the benefits of the free market and the "invisible hand" of capitalism still hold much sway in modern economic thought. Indeed, the capitalist economic system of the United States is largely influenced by Smith. But though capitalism is associated with the pursuit of profit and wealth, Smith's concern was not just about the best way to get rich. Smith was concerned with how economics—and a fair economic system—might help ordinary people lead better lives. Smith's view of people was ultimately an optimistic one, and he truly believed that given the freedom to follow their own self-interest, in response to market incentives, people would act in the best interest of all.

Time Line

1723: Born in Kirkcaldy, Scotland.

1733: Enrolls in Kirkcaldy Burgh School.

1737: Enrolls in University of Glasgow at age fourteen.

1740: Begins studies at Balliol College at Cambridge to become a minister.

1746: Returns to Kirkcaldy.

1748: Moves to Edinburgh to give public lectures.

1751: Becomes professor at University of Glasgow.

1759: Publishes *The Theory of Moral Sentiments*.

1764: Begins travels to England, France, and Switzerland to educate the Duke of Buccleuch; begins writing *The Wealth of Nations*.

1767: Returns to Kirkcaldy and continues writing *The Wealth of Nations*.

1776: Publishes *The Wealth of Nations*.

1778: Appointed comptroller of customs of Scotland in Edinburgh, Scotland.

1790: Dies at age 67.

Source Notes

1: The Young Smith

p. 6, "constitution during infancy . . ." Dugald Stewart, *Account of the Life and Writings of Adam Smith LL.D*, vol. 10, Collected Works of Dugald Stewart (Edinburgh: Thomas Constable and Co., 1854), 5.

p. 20, "by no means one of . . ." Adam Smith, *An Inquiry Into the Nature and Causes of The Wealth of Nations* (Indianapolis: Liberty Fund, 1981), 18.

p. 20, "attracted notice, by his passion . . ." Stewart, *Account of the Life and Writings of Adam Smith LL.D*, 6.

p. 21, "She was blamed . . ." Ibid., 5–6.

3: To Oxford and the Ministry

p. 44, "his health at Oxford . . ." Ernest Campbell Mossner and Ian Simpson Ross, eds., *The Correspondence of Adam Smith* (London: Clarendon Press, 1987), 1.

p. 44, "The endowments of schools . . ." Smith, *An Inquiry Into the Nature and Causes of The Wealth of Nations*, 760.

p. 44, "In the University of Oxford . . ." Ibid., 761.

p. 46, "I think of you . . ." Mossner and Ross, *The Correspondence of Adam Smith*, 3.

4: Scholarly Beginnings

p. 54, "I should prefer David Hume . . ." Mossner and Ross, *The Correspondence of Adam Smith*, 5.

p. 58, "Did you ever hear of . . ." Ibid., 20.

p. 59, "has had the imprudence . . ." Ibid., 21.

p. 60, "Fitzmaurice attends . . ." Ibid., 28.

p. 60, "He attends different Masters . . ." Ibid., 29.

5: The Theory of Moral Sentiments

p. 64, "nasty, brutish, and short," Thomas Hobbes, *Leviathan* (London: Cambridge University Press, 1904), 84.

p. 64, "so odious . . ." Adam Smith, *The Theory of Moral Sentiments* (Indianapolis: Liberty Fund, 1982), 318.

p. 65, "The disposition to the affections . . ." Ibid., 243.

p. 65, "may sometimes be . . ." Ibid.

p. 65, "the mind was naturally . . ." Ibid., 318

p. 65, "when in our hearts . . ." Ibid., 44.

p. 65, "Men are qualified . . ." Jerry Z. Muller, *Adam Smith in His Time and Ours* (Princeton: Princeton University Press, 1993), 99.

p. 66, "Every man is, no doubt . . ." Smith, *The Theory of Moral Sentiments*, 82.

p. 67, "How selfish soever . . ." Ibid., 9.

p. 67, "The desire of becoming . . ." Ibid., 213.

p. 67, "As we have no immediate . . ." Ibid., 9.

p. 68, "It is so disagreeable . . ." Ibid., 158.

p. 68, "The fundamental principle . . ." Stewart, *Account of the Life and Writings of Adam Smith LL.D*, 17.

p. 68, "The principle by which we naturally either approve . . ." Smith, *The Theory of Moral Sentiments*, 109.

p. 69, "are fond of deducing . . ." Ibid., 13.

p. 69, "Man naturally desires, not only to be loved . . ." Ibid., 113–114.

p. 69, "When we have read a book . . ." Ibid., 14.

p. 69, "No benevolent man ever lost . . ." Ibid., 225.

p. 70,   "the cleverest Fellow . . ." Mossner and Ross, *The Correspondence of Adam Smith*, 36.

p. 74,   "the plan of his . . ." Stewart, *Account of the Life and Writings of Adam Smith LL.D*, 42.

p. 74,   "It is probable, that the uninterrupted . . ." Ibid..

p. 74,   "could not depart . . ." Mossner and Ross, *The Correspondence of Adam Smith*, 91.

6: Travels Abroad

p. 75,   "cleverest Fellow . . ." Mossner and Ross, *The Correspondence of Adam Smith*, 36.

p. 78,   "I have begun to write . . ." Ibid., 102.

p. 85,   "I have now Opulence . . ." Ibid., 106.

p. 87,   "By endeavouring to unmask . . ." Ibid., 113.

p. 87,   "He vomited, but not enough . . ." Ibid., 114.

7: From Kirkcaldy to London

p. 91,   "What has become of . . ." Mossner and Ross, *The Correspondence of Adam Smith*, 125.

p. 91,   "very ill us'd . . ." Ibid., 126.

p. 91,   "broke for ever." Ibid.

p. 92,   "I cannot easily express . . ." Ibid., 131–132.

p. 92,   "I thank you for . . ." Ibid., 133.

p. 96,   "As I have left the care . . ." Ibid., 168.

p. 101, "How is it suppos'd . . ." Ibid., 171.

p. 103, "I am as lazy a Correspondent . . ." Ibid., 185–186.

p. 104, "Euge! Belle! . . ." Ibid., 186.

p. 105, "This is a Diarrhea . . ." Ibid., 191.

p. 106, "died in such a happy . . ." Ibid., 209.

8: The Wealth of Nations

p. 107, "Servants, labourers, and workmen . . ." Smith, *An Inquiry Into the Nature and Causes of The Wealth of Nations*, 96.

p. 108, "Consumption is the sole end . . ." Ibid., 660.

p. 108, "that wealth does not consist . . ." Ibid., 438.

p. 110, "The greatest improvement . . ." Ibid., 13.

p. 110, "One man draws out the wire . . ." Ibid., 15.

p. 110, "make among them upwards . . . pin in a day," Ibid.

p. 111, "great increase of the quantity . . ." Ibid., 17.

p. 111, "first, to the increase of dexterity . . ." Ibid.

p. 111, "When the market is very small . . ." Ibid., 31.

p. 114, "When the quantity brought to market . . ." Ibid., 74.

p. 114, "is neither more nor less . . ." Ibid., 72.

p. 114, "If in the same neighbourhood . . ." Ibid., 116.

p. 114, "intends only his own gain . . ." Ibid., 456.

p. 115, "The statesman, who should . . ." Ibid.

p. 115, "Observe the accommodation . . ." Ibid., 22.

p. 116, "coarse and rough," Ibid.

p. 116, "day-labourer," Ibid.

p. 116, "It is not from the benevolence . . ." Ibid., 26–27.

p. 117, "By means of glasses, hotbeds, and . . ." Ibid., 458.

p. 118, "The interest of a nation in . . ." Ibid., 464.

p. 119, "Humanity may in this . . . " Ibid., 469.

p. 119, "In every country it . . ." Ibid., 493.

p. 119, "directly opposite to that . . ." Ibid., 494.

p. 120, "in the system of laws which . . ." Ibid., 661.

p. 120, "give up all authority over . . ." Ibid., 616.

p. 120, "Great Britain would not only . . ." Ibid., 617.

9: An Advocate for Free Trade

p. 125, "Among the strange report . . ." Mossner and Ross, *The Correspondence of Adam Smith*, 228.

p. 127, "It is in consequence of . . ." Smith, *An Inquiry Into the Nature and Causes of The Wealth of Nations*, 495.

p. 127, "I cannot believe a . . ." Mossner and Ross, *The Correspondence of Adam Smith*, 243.

p. 128, "I should think it . . ." Ibid., 242.

p. 128, "I am ashamed of . . ." Ibid., 249–250.

p. 131, "I have many apologies to . . ." Ibid., 263.

p. 132, "You have made a . . ." Ibid., 232.

p. 132, "I think it is predestined that . . ." Ibid., 248–249.

p. 133, "I intended to have asked . . ." Ibid., 269.

10: The Author of *The Wealth of Nations* Lies Here

p. 134, "I must say to you . . ." Mossner and Ross, *The Correspondence of Adam Smith*, 275.

p. 136, "My friends grow very thin . . ." Ibid., 275.

p. 137, "I accept with gratitude . . ." Ibid., 308–309.

p. 138, "I expected by this time . . ." Ibid., 325.

p. 139, "I am a slow . . ." Ibid., 311.

Bibliography

Aldridge, Alfred Owen. *Benjamin Franklin: Philosopher and Man*. New York: J. P. Lippincott Company, 1965.

Anderson, Gary M., et al. "Adam Smith in the Custom House." *Journal of Political Economy* 93, no. 4 (August 1985): 740–759.

Ashraf, Nava, et al. "Adam Smith, Behavioral Economist." *Journal of Economic Perspectives* 19, no. 3 (Summer 2005): 131–145.

Bayne-Powell, Rosamond. *Eighteenth-Century London Life*. New York: E.P. Dutton & Co., Inc., 1938.

Bourne, H.R. Fox. *The Life of John Locke*, Vol. I and Vol. II. London, England: Henry S. King & Co., 1876.

Brands, H.W. *The First American: The Life and Times of Benjamin Franklin*. New York: Doubleday, 2000.

Broadie, Alexander. *The Scottish Enlightenment: The Historical Age of the Historical Nation*. Edinburgh, Scotland: Birlinn Limited, 2001.

Brown, Louise Fargo. *The First Earl of Shaftesbury*. New York: D. Appleton-Century Company, Inc., 1933.

Buchanan, James. "Adam Smith as Inspiration." *The Collected Works of James M. Buchanan: "Ideas, Persons, and Events."* Liberty Fund, Indianapolis, Indiana, (2001): 289–303.

———. "The Justice of Natural Liberty." *Journal of Legal Studies* 5, no. 1 (Jan 1976): 1–6.

Buchholz, Todd G. *New Ideas from Dead Economists: An Introduction to Modern Economic Thought*. New York: The Penguin Group, 1989.

Bussing-Burks, Marie. *Influential Economists*. Minneapolis, Minnesota: The Oliver Press, Inc., 2003.

Campbell, Lord Archibald. *Highland Dress, Arms and Ornament*, London, England: Archibald Constable & Co., 1899. Reprinted 1969, London, England: Dawsons of Pall Mall.

Campbell, R. H., and A. S. Skinner. *Adam Smith*. New York, St. Martin's Press, 1982.

"Charles Townsend." Reference Encyclopedia. www.reference.com/browse/wiki/charles_townshend

Chernow, Ron. *Alexander Hamilton*. New York: The Penguin Press, 2004.

Cohen, I. Bernard. *Science and the Founding Fathers*. New York: W. W. Norton & Company, Inc., 1995.

Cunnington, Phyllis. *Costumes of the Seventeenth and Eighteenth Century*. Boston, MA: Plays Inc., 1970.

Dankert, Clyde E. *Thoughts from Adam Smith*. Vermont: Stinehour Press, 1963.

Dumas, Malone. *Jefferson and His Time: The Sage of Monticello*. Boston: Little, Brown and Company, 1981.

Dunbar, John Telfer. *The Costume of Scotland*. London, England: B.T. Batsford Ltd., 1981.

Evensky, Jerry. "Adam Smith's Theory of Moral Sentiments: On Morals and Why They Matter to a Liberal Society of Free people and Free Markets." *Journal of Economic Perspectives* 19, no. 3 (Summer 2005): 109–130.

———. "Chicago Smith Versus Kirkcaldy Smith." *History of Political Economy* 37, no. 2 (Summer 2005): 197–203.

Farrand, Max. *The Framing of the Constitution of the United States*. New Haven: Yale University Press, 1913.

Fay, C.R. *Adam Smith and the Scotland of His Day*. Cambridge, England: Cambridge University press, 1956.

Foner, Eric. *Tom Paine and Revolutionary America*. New York: Oxford University Press, 1976.

Friedman, Milton. "Economists and Economic Policy." *Economic Inquiry* 24, no. 1 (Jan 1986): 1–10.

Friedman, Milton, and Rose Friedman. *Free to Choose: A Personal Statement*. California, San Diego: A Harvest Book, Harcourt, Inc, 1980.

Gilbreath, James, and Douglas L. Wilson, eds. *Thomas Jefferson's Library: A Catalog with Entries in His Own Order*. Washington, D.C.: Library of Congress, 1989.

Graham, Henry Grey. *Social Life of Scotland in the Eighteenth Century*. London: Adam and Charles Black, 1909.

Griswold, Charles L. Jr. *Adam Smith and the Virtues of Enlightenment*. Cambridge, United Kingdom: Cambridge University Press, 1999.

Haggarty, John. *The Wisdom of Adam Smith: A Collection of His Most Incisive and Eloquent Observations*. Indianapolis, Indiana: Liberty Fund, 1976.

Hamowy, Ronald. "Jefferson and the Scottish Enlightenment: A Critique of Garry Wills's Inventing America—Jefferson's Declaration of Independence." *William and Mary Quarterly*, no. 36 (Oct 1979): 503–523.

Heilbroner, Robert L. *The Worldly Philosophers: The Lives, Times, and Ideas of the Great Economic Thinkers*, 7th ed. New York: Simon & Schuster, 1999.

Heilbroner, Robert L., and Laurence J. Malone, eds. *The Essential Adam Smith*. New York: W.W. Norton & Company, 1986.

Herman, Author. *How the Scots Invented the Modern World*. New York: Crown Publishers, 2001.

Hobbes, Thomas. *Leviathan*. London: Cambridge University Press, 1904.

Hofstadter, Richard. *The American Political Tradition, and the Men Who Made It*. New York: Alfred A. Knopf, 1989.

Hume, David. *Essays: Moral, Political, and Literary*. Edited and with a Foreword, Notes, and Glossary by Eugene F. Miller. Indianapolis, Indiana: Liberty Fund, 1987.

Kalyvas, Andreas, and Ira Katznelson. "The Rhetoric of the Market: Adam Smith on Recognitions, Speech, and Exchange." *Review of Politics* 63, no. 3 (Summer): 549–579.

Kronenwetter, Michael. *Are You a Liberal? Are You a Conservative?* New York: Franklin Watts, 1984.

McCullough, David. *John Adams*. New York: Simon and Schuster, 2001.

McGuinness, Arthur E. *Henry Home, Lord Kames*. New York: Twayne Publishers, Inc., 1970.

Mossner, Ernest Campbell and Ian Simpson Ross, eds. *The Correspondence of Adam Smith*. 2nd ed. Oxford, England: Clarendon Press, 1987.

Muller, Jerry Z. *Adam Smith in His Time and Ours*. Princeton, New Jersey: Princeton University Press, 1993.

Omand, Donald. *The Fife Book*. Edinburgh, Scotland: Birlinn Limited, 2000.

Paine, Thomas. *Common Sense, 1776*. Edited with an Introduction by Isaac Kramnick. New York: Penguin Books, 1983.

Poole, J. R. *Foundations of American Independence: 1763–1815*. New York: The Bobbs-Merrill Company, Inc., 1972.

Rae, John. *Life of Adam Smith*, London: Macmillan and Co., 1895. Reprinted 1967, Fairfield, New Jersey: Augustus M. Kelley. With an introduction, "Guide to John Rae's Life of Adam Smith," by Jacob Viner.

Razeen, Sally. "David Hume, Adam Smith, and the Scottish Enlightenment." *Society* 36, no. 2 (Jan-Feb 1999): 41–44.

Rogers, Charles. *Social Life in Scotland from Early to Recent Times, Vol. I and Vol. II*, 1884 ed. Port Washington, New York: Kennikat Press, 1971.

Rogers, G. A. J. *Locke's Enlightenment: Aspects of the Origin, Nature and Impact of his Philosophy*. New York: Georg Olms AG, 1998.

Rogge, Benjamin A. *Can Capitalism Survive?* Library of Economics and Liberty, http://www.econlib.org/library/LFBooks/Rogge/rggCCS3.html

Rosenberg, Nathan, and L.E. Birdzell, Jr. *How the West Grew Rich: The Economic Transformation of the Industrial World*. U.S.A.: Basic Books, Inc., 1986.

Ross, Ian Simpson. *The Life of Adam Smith*. Oxford, England: Oxford University Press, 1995.

Rothbard, Murray N. "The Adam Smith Myth." Posted by the Mises Institute (January 13, 2006) at www.mises.org/story/2012. Excerpt from *An Austrian Perspective on the History of Economic Thought*, Edward Edgar author, Vol. I and II (1995).

Ryan, Edward W. *In the Words of Adam Smith: The First Consumer Advocate*. Sun Lakes, Arizona: Thomas Horton and Daughters, 1990.

Samuels, Warren J., and Steven G. Medema. "Freeing Smith from the 'Free Market': On the Misperception of Adam Smith on the Economic Role of Government." *History of Political Economy* 37, no. 2 (Summer 2005): 219–226.

Schliesser, Eric. "The Obituary of a Vain Philosopher: Adam Smith's Reflections on Hume's Life." *Hume Studies* 29, no. 2 (November 2003): 327–362.

Schumpeter, Joseph A. *History of Economic Analysis*, 5th ed. New York: University Press, 1963.

Schwartz, Richard B. *Daily Life in Johnson's London*. Madison, Wisconsin: The University of Wisconsin Press, 1983.

Scott, Jonathan. *Algernon Sidney and the English Republic, 1623–1677*. New York: Cambridge University Press, 1988.

———. *Algernon Sidney and the Restoration Crisis, 1677–1683*. New York: Cambridge University Press, 1991.

Scott, William Robert. *Adam Smith as Student and Professor*. New York: Augustus M. Kelley, 1965.

———. *Francis Hutcheson: His Life, Teaching and Position in the History of Philosophy*. New York: Augustus M. Kelley, 1966.

Smith, Adam. *An Inquiry Into the Nature and Causes of The Wealth of Nations*, Vol. I and Vol. II, 1979 ed., reprint authorized by Oxford University Press. Indianapolis, Indiana: Liberty Fund, 1981.

———. *The Theory of Moral Sentiments*. 1979 ed., reprint authorized by Oxford University Press. Indianapolis, Indiana: Liberty Fund, 1982.

Smith, Roy C. *Adam Smith and the Origins of American Enterprise*. New York: St. Martin's Press, 2002.

Smout, T. C. *A History of the Scottish People, 1560–1830*. St. James's Place, London: Collins, 1969.

Stewart, Dugald. *Account of the Life and Writings of Adam Smith LL.D.* Printed in *The Collected Works of Dugald Stewart*, vol. 10, 1–98. Edinburgh: Thomas Constable and Co., 1854.

———. *Biographical Memoir of Smith LL.D.*, 1793. Reprinted 1966, Edited by Sir William Hamilton, Bart. Fairfield, New Jersey: Augustus M. Kelley.

Stigler, George J. "The Successes and Failures of Professor Smith." *Journal of Political Economy* 84, no. 6 (1976): 1199–1213.

West, E. G. *Adam Smith: The Man and His Works*. Indianapolis, Indiana: Liberty Fund, 1976.

Wiegand, Wayne A., and Donald G. Davis, eds. *Encyclopedia of Library History*. New York: Garland Publishing, 1994.

Web Sites

http://www.adamsmith.org

Web site of the Adam Smith Institute, a British economic think tank named for the famous economist. Features essays and articles about economics, a biography of Smith, and list of Smith's notable quotes.

http://www.econlib.org

The Web site of the Library of Economics and Liberty features various articles, blogs, and resources about economics, both in history and today. Visitors also will find an online edition of *The Theory of Moral Sentiments* (sixth edition) and *An Inquiry into the Nature and Causes of the Wealth of Nations* (fifth edition).

Index

Numbers in **bold italics** refer to captions.

Picture Credits